IMAGININGS

IMAGININGS

An Addendum

to

Important Things

JOHN E. BEERBOWER

PREFACE

These essays are on topics reflecting the intersection of science and humankind. They concern time, consciousness, beauty, probability, free will and understanding. They supplement and compliment my book *Important Things We Don't Know (About Nearly Everything)* and are presented here as an accompaniment to that book. But, this volume can stand on its own.

For several years, I periodically updated *Important Things*. But, I decided to leave the last edition as the last. Yet, I keep reading and thinking. So, I have been writing short essays on scientific subjects and including them in my *Wanderings* books. There are now enough that I thought it worth making them (updated and revised—in some cases, very substantially), along with several new ones, available as an addendum to the original book.

Many of these essays assume familiarity with material in my first book, *Important Things*. That book contains contextual background that I do not repeat. Of course, many readers may already know enough science to follow the discussions herein.

CONTENTS

Introduction

In 2016, I wrote:

"...Carl Sagan, prophesized in 1979 that the process of discovery was almost complete:

'This book is written just before—at most, I believe, a few years or a few decades before—the answers to many of these vexing and awesome questions on origins and fates are pried loose from the cosmos.

...Had we been born fifty years later, the answers would, I think, already have been in... .

'[I]n all of the four-billion-year history of life on our planet, in all of the four-million-year history of the human family, there is only one generation privileged to live through that unique transitional moment: that generation is ours.' Broca's Brain: Reflections on the Romance of Science (1979), p.xv.

"I am, in fact, of that very generation of which Sagan wrote and, of course, we are now almost four decades into the future that he was imagining. Yet, this book today discusses most of the same 'fundamental' and 'awesome questions' to which Sagan had referred.

"In his words:

> '...[Q]uestions on the origins of consciousness; life on our planet; the beginnings of the Earth; the formation of the Sun; the possibility of intelligent beings somewhere up there in the depths of the sky; as well as, the grandest inquiry of all—on the advent, nature and ultimate destiny of the universe.' *Id.*, p.xiii.

"As you might have guessed, the answers are not yet in. Not even close. You younger readers were not, in fact, born too late to experience the wonder and mystery or to partake of the process of discovery. Indeed, I believe that the same will be true for your children (and theirs)."

Limits of Science? Important things we do not know about nearly everything (2016), p.19; *Important Things We Don't Know* (2022), p.xvii.

* * *

In 2023, astrophysicist Lawrence Krauss, whose first book—*A Universe from Nothing: Why There is Something Rather Than Nothing* (2012)—I had cited repeatedly, published a book entitled *The Edge of Knowledge: Unsolved Mysteries of the Cosmos* (2023) (Kindle).

It begins:

"Three of the most important words in science are: 'I don't know.' Therein lies the beginning of enlightenment because not knowing implies a universe of opportunities— the possibility of discovery and of surprise."

So, it appears that my views have become mainstream.

Curiously, I also then wrote (p.427): "[I]n language reminiscent of Carl Sagan's misplaced excitement about living at the crucial point in biological sciences ..., Lawrence Krause [sic] speculated that we may be in the very unique and fortunate position of being able to predict the future, because of the current relationship between dark energy and the density of matter in the Universe, and to understand the past in ways that would not have been possible a few billion years ago and will again not be possible a few billion years hence. *Id.* pp.117–9, 121–6."

But, has anything fundamental changed about the "things we don't know" in the seven years?

Here is Krauss' recent (2023) list (loc.72):

"How did our universe begin, if it even had a beginning? How will it end? How big is it? What lies beyond what we can see? What are the fundamental laws governing our existence? Are those laws the same everywhere? What is the world of our experience made of? What remains hidden? How did life on earth arise? Are we alone? What is consciousness? Is human consciousness unique?"

It seems not.

So, onward.

Time

CHAPTER 2

Timelessness, Eternity and Us

I have written several dozens of pages on the meaning and nature of time, but I still feel something is missing. So, I offer some more thoughts on timelessness, eternity and us.

When we examine, discuss or even think about time, we effectively step outside of time and make it an object.

TIMELESS

Start with what we mean by eternal. It can be used to refer to endless time, time without end. It is also used to refer to timelessness, somehow outside of time. Modern cosmology assures us that the Universe is not eternal, that it will have an end. Some physicists conclude, therefore, that time must also have an end. However, if time has an end, then it almost certainly has a beginning. (The arguable consistency between that conclusion and certain religious beliefs bothers some scientists, but that is a different matter.) So, if time is not endless, can anything be timeless, or is that just an expression we use, like "timeless beauty"?

Well, we often talk about mathematics as being timeless, as being always true and unchanging (*i.e.*, eternal). Arguably, the same could be said about logic more generally and, indeed, about theoretical science. What we mean is that mathematics is not dependent upon time, it is not affected by time, it is not temporal. We can say it exists outside of time. Likewise, classical science is based on the premise that there exist Laws of Nature that are eternal in both senses of the word—everlasting and independent or outside of time. We may only know approximations of those Laws, but we believe they exist and that we can come closer and closer to discovering them. That is what science is about.

In addition, we imagine eternity. We routinely contemplate the future. And, the past. We exercise our imagination in all sorts of ways. None of these things are time dependent, like causal relationships (the cause necessarily preceding the effect in time). Of course, we do all of these things "in time", but that is a different concept.

Other examples of timelessness can be found even in the physical world, according to theoretical physics. Einstein's General Theory characterizes the physical world as existing in four dimensional space-time in which travel in the four dimensions is subject to a universal speed limit, generally assumed to be the speed of light. Thus, when light is traveling through three dimensional space (at the speed of light, naturally), it can not be traveling through time, *i.e.*, it is necessarily timeless. It does not age; it is eternal. The same would be true for any and all things that are traveling at the speed of light!. But, you might say, it takes light 8 minutes to travel to the Earth from the moon, so isn't that light 8 minutes older? No, it has not aged. It is the very same light that originated earlier, just being observed later.

(Similarly, an object that is completely motionless in three dimensional space will be traveling only through time. This implication is somewhat ambiguous given the assumption in Einstein's Special

Theory that there is no absolute space, so one cannot know that the object is actually motionless.)

Indeed, the one-way flow of time is simply not part of most of modern physics. Perhaps, the passage of time simply is not part of physical reality. We experience it profoundly, but that may be a purely human phenomenon. The passage of time may be an integral part of how we think and perceive the world, but perhaps it is not part of the world outside of us.

However, "[w]henever a physical process is not in a state of equilibrium, time enters into the equation. It is always possible to distinguish a before and an after, which we can't do with systems in equilibrium." Giorgio Parisi, In a *Flight of Starlings: The Wonders of Complex Systems* (2023), p.79.

So, timelessness is not such a rare characteristic after all. Furthermore, physicists tell us that the elemental particles, as well as many types of atoms, will exist unchanging forever. Thus, it is said that the stuff of our bodies comes from the stars and will return to the stars. Matter and energy, it seems, are eternal.

ETERNAL

But, "the eternal" is still an essentially human phenomenon; it exists because we exist.

Some physical aspects of eternity may be present, but it is only through human awareness that is it realized. Just like time itself. Color and sound may exist without us, because animals can see and hear. But, not eternity. It is only human beings with our unique awareness of, and anticipation of, death that perceive timelessness. We bring the eternal into the world.

> "The knowledge of death is the awareness of a time longer than the period allotted to me: of a time 'before' and 'after' my life... . The power that allows me to conceive a time longer than my life throws the brevity of my existence into painful relief. ...It allows us to consider the world and ourselves from **a vantage point other animals can never attain**. ...[T]he uncanny power to see that we are living in time, as opposed to merely doing so ... ."

Anthony T. Kronman, *After Disbelief: On Disenchantment, Disappointment, Eternity, and Joy* (2022), pp.30, 32 (emphasis added). *

If we are what brings the eternal into our world, what else does our existence do? Is there something more we can say about our role?

HUMAN

I have written elsewhere about the nature of Consciousness, the Anthropic Principle, the Fine-tuning Problem and our (human's) Role in the Universe. I have previously noted how humans (as conscious, self-reflective entities) introduced awe, joy and beauty into the Universe; that a star might have always emitted electromagnetic waves, but only with the presence of we humans does it "shine" and "twinkle." I want to take those speculations a step further.

Take the question: "Why is there something rather than nothing?" One answer is: "Because we exist." The reason that is an answer to the question is that if we did not exist, then the question would never be asked. Now, this example seems a bit gimmicky. Like a word game.

Then, there is the quantum mechanics view:

"The distinguished theoretical physicist John Wheeler... took the conscious-dependent view of physical reality to its logical conclusion. He argued that the universe depends for its existence on the presence of conscious observers to make it real, not only today but also retrospectively to the Big Bang. The universe existed in a kind of indeterminate probabilistic ghost state until conscious beings observed it, thus collapsing the wave function for the entire universe and bringing it into physical existence."

John Hands, *Cosmosapiens: Human Evolution from the Origin of the Universe* (2016), pp. 87-8.

But, I am thinking of something different, although possibly related.

Take another example.

We can assert that since we exist, the Universe has to be the way it is (because if it were not, we would not). We might also plausibly assert that because we exist, the Universe is as it is. This formulation carries a different implication. It suggests causation. Not causality as we normally understand it, with its mandatory temporal implications; but, causality pursuant to what is called a "teleological" explanation. The goal or function to be achieved causes the circumstances necessary to its realization. Somehow, it pulls along everything else in order to make the appearance of the desired result, not only possible, but actual.

Alternatively, there are tendencies toward certain end results that influence how things are, moving the world towards those ends. Indeed, visions of the future shape the here-and-now. The preexisting function or goal is the reason the Universe is as it is. Because we humans with consciousness exist, the Universe must be as it is and, also, is why it is as it is. In order for us to be here, the Universe was created; it was created for that purpose.

Is this argument subject to the same characterization as the prior example—rather gimmicky?

Not for me.

MAYBE

The status of teleological explanations—that things happen for (because of) a reason or objective—is hotly debated. For obvious reasons, it is rejected, even loathed, by most scientists, but the views of philosophers are more mixed. The problem is the suggestion of intention. This type of explanation works well for human creations—the object is as it is because that is what its creator wanted, it is that way because of the function it was intended to perform, its function is why it looks as it does or is as it is.

However, intention is not a necessary part of teleology.

There is certainly evidence of the acceptance, and even the embrace, of such explanations by earlier civilizations. Indeed, teleology is at the heart of Aristotle's metaphysics. It also appears in the works of Kant, Hegel and Marx. And, "there is disagreement as to whether or not Darwin's evolutionary explanations are teleological. Even Darwin's contemporaries disagreed ... ." Colin Allen and Neal Jacob, "Teleological Notions in Biology," *The Stanford Encyclopedia of Philosophy* (Spring 2020 Edition).

"In any case, it is clear that Darwin used the language of 'final causes' to describe the function of biological parts in his Species Notebooks and throughout his life; he also reflected frequently about the relationship between natural selection and teleology." *Id.*

Or, perhaps, self-reflective consciousness was somehow built into the fabric of the Universe at the beginning, as a part of the creation itself, so we are an inevitable part of evolution. "[O]nce it has emerged from the inorganic, life continues naturally, and in a combined twofold movement, to become both [more complex] externally and more conscious internally; and this extends up to the psychological emergence of reflection." Pierre Teilhard de Chardin, *Christianity and Evolution: Reflections on Science and Religion*, p.230.

The real question is not whether we find such explanations to be illuminating, but whether they actually capture any part of reality. But, to find evidence of that, we must have our eyes open, open to the possibility.

We need to be willing to expand our minds.

---

* I wrote this essay shortly after reading *After Disbelief:* I have borrowed the starting point, the two meanings of eternal. There are also a few similarities in what follows, but I do not find many of his arguments nor his conclusions to be persuasive, and I end in a different place.

CHAPTER 3

"Turn, Turn, Turn"

"To everything
(Turn! Turn! Turn!)
There is a season
(Turn! Turn! Turn!)
And a time to every purpose,
under Heaven"

Pete Seeger (1959), The Byrds (1965)

"We inhabit time as fish live in water.

...

"Do we exist in time, or does time exist in us?"

Carlo Rovelli
The Order of Time, pp.1, 3.

I find that my mind keeps wandering back to wonder what time really is. Carlo Rovelli declares: "The nature of time is perhaps the greatest remaining mystery." *The Order of Time* (2016), p.2. So it seems to me. I have written at length about all of the things we still do not understand about our world, but in most areas, one feels we are at least on the right trail to the answer. With respect to time, however, I feel we are just flailing. (Excuse the mixed metaphor.) However, as Rovelli observes: "We are not even clear about what it means 'to understand.' We see the world and we describe it: we give it an order. We know little of the actual relation between what we see of the world and the world itself. We know that we are myopic." *Id.*, p.210.

In 2017, I made limited use of Rovelli's book because he seemed too far from the main stream. Quantum gravitational theory, after all! But, I have gone back and reread it. Here is what I have concluded.

We can think of time as the process of aging. On our scale, everything ages; although, the relative "rate" of the aging will vary based on relative speed of travel and gravity. Aging consists of the conversion of mass to energy, energy to heat, dispersion of heat (from hot to cold) and the decrease in order (increase in disorder or entropy). Aging is a process that affects (or occurs in connection with) everything that is "ordered." Ordered things require the injection of energy to be maintained. The new energy combats the tendency to disorder. Such a system will not be in equilibrium.

There is no universal or absolute time. It is a purely local phenomenon, occurring or appearing in particular places. If, in the beginning, something is highly ordered (very low entropy), then the process of time is inevitable. "If we observe a phenomenon that begins in a state of lower entropy, it is clear why entropy increases—because in the process of reshuffling, everything becomes disordered." *Id.*, p.31. Otherwise, there is no time.

So, we say that our Universe necessarily began in a state of extremely low entropy, because time passes (and, because time passes, there must have been a beginning). But, we come face to face with the question of why entropy was so low in the beginning. We are back to "The Fine-Tuning Problem," only with one more inexplicable condition, and a very big one. Our Universe **had** to be in a state of very low entropy in the beginning for us to exist now.

Rovelli tries to ameliorate this condition through the weak form of the Anthropic Principle. He postulates that it may be only in one or some parts of the Universe where time exists (a "subset"). In an infinite Universe with random configurations, there will be some configurations that just happen to have low entropy. *See id.*, pp.144-9. (Remember, "anything that can happen does happen.") And, of course, for us to live, we must be in one of them.

And, the low-entropy spaces? Just random events?

"The Creator gave the universe time. **Time not only brought change and progres**s, but also gave low-entropy entities existence. Time and the absolute-limit speed are two sides of the same blade that divided the universe, isolating most species of low-entropy entities and their civilizations in **tiny corners of the vast cosmos.**"

Baoshu, *The Redemption of Time* (2016), p.200 (emphasis added).

But, the causal relationship is likely reversed. Low-entropy spaces probably created time locally, not *vice versa*.

We have no evidence of and can imagine no experiment to test this hypothesis. And, in fact, it appears that entropy is increasing in the entire visible Universe. Indeed, Rovelli himself goes on to discuss time as if the whole Universe is involved.

We understand that at the level of elementary particles, things do not age. But, stuff happens. Things, or maybe just "fields," vibrate, move and change relationships with one another. Yet, there is no time.

> "If I observe the microscopic state of things, then the difference between past and future vanishes. The future of the world, for instance, is determined by its present state—though neither more nor less than is the past. We often say that causes precede effects and yet, in the elementary grammar of things, there is no distinction between 'cause' and 'effect.'"

Rovelli, *The Order of Time*, pp.32-3.

So, if we were to observe at that scale, we would be unable to see "the forest for the trees." From our vantage point, of course, we see only the "forest", and we see the seasons change. Therefore, does time only exist on our scale?

If so, is it, then, an emergent property of the macroscopic?

Although Rovelli uses the word "emerge" frequently, he is not really referring to "emergence," as I have discussed it elsewhere. Certainly not "strong emergence." He asserts that the elements that constitute time exist everywhere, even though "time" may not.

"In a world without time, there must still be something that gives rise to the time that we are accustomed to, with its order, with its past that is different from the future, with its smooth flowing. Somehow, our time must emerge around us, at least for us and at our scale." *Id.* p.5.

Perhaps, then, the explanation is that time is observable only at a certain scale or from certain perspectives, like the forest. It exists everywhere, but it can only be perceived in certain places. Rovelli stresses the importance of point of view.

> "If we give a description of the world that ignores point of view, that is solely 'from the outside—of space, of time, of a subject—we may be able to say many things but we lose certain crucial aspects of the world. Because the world that we have been given is the world seen from within it, not from without. Many things that we see in the world can be understood only if we take into account the role played by point of view. ...We must not, in short, confuse the temporal structures that belong to the world as 'seen from the outside' with the aspects of the world that we observe and which depend on our being part of it, on our being situated within it."

Id., p.153.

Surely, in this he is correct.

But, he also tries to tie perspective into physical relationships (actually, interactions) and his theory of entropy. Those speculations, I do not buy.

Rovelli cites well known thinkers who suggested that time was internal to mankind or not "real": Leibniz, Wittgenstein, Kant, Aristotle and St. Augustine.

But, again, I think he is proposing something different.

He writes:

> "The entropy of the world in the far past appears very low to us. But this might not reflect the exact state of the world: **it might regard the subset of the world's variables with which we, as physical systems, have interacted.** ...[Perhaps] it wasn't the universe that was in a very particular configuration in the past. **Perhaps instead it is us, and our interactions with the universe, that are particular.** We are the ones who determine a particular macroscopic description. The initial low entropy of the universe, and hence the arrow of time, may be more down to us than to the universe itself. ...Perhaps, therefore, the flow of time is not a characteristic of the universe: **like the rotation of the heavens, it is due to the particular perspective that we have from our corner of it.**"

Id., pp.146-8, 150 (emphasis added).

In *Important Things*, I discussed three alternative interpretations of time: that it is an illusion, is a fundamental element of the Universe or is purely a human phenomenon. Seven years ago, I was inclined to the fundamental. But, now I perceive time as not fundamental, as used therein, but more as coincidental, to physics. Something that can happen. As to the perception of time, I see that as a phenomenon created by memory combined with consciousness. (Whether other animals have the requisite combination to experience time is an interesting question.) Past, present and future. What we live by. The past, with our memory; the future with our consciousness. The present? A bit complicated. To some extent, with our subconscious.

"One of the problems is that each memory is the memory of the memory before. You cant remember the occasion of the actual memory. How would you do that? You just remember remembering it. And only the most recent memory at that." Cormac McCarthy, *Stella Maris* (2022), p.39.

Yes, time may be a distinctly human phenomenon, arising from our particular position of observation. It is always there (at least, where entropy has not reached a maximum), but it is not always relevant. Except for us. It is embedded in, and integral to, the way our brains experience and relate to the world in terms of past, present and future.

Without us to experience it, perhaps time would not exist.

Yet,

Remember, while we "know" that time is relative to each observer, we have concluded that it is affected both by speed and by gravity. (Einstein's thought experiment allowing time to vary among observers—although, not empirically established until later—addressed a real physics problem at the time.)

"The theory of electromagnetism had just been fully exposited by the great theoretical physicist James Clerk Maxwell only forty years earlier, based on the groundbreaking work of the equally great experimental physicist Michael Faraday. Maxwell's theory predicted that light is a wave of electromagnetic fields whose speed is determined by two fundamental constants of nature: the strength of electricity and the strength of magnetism. These constants reflect the underlying properties of space itself, and therefore they should be measured to have the same value for all observers. Einstein recognized that Maxwell's result would imply that all observers would have to measure light as having the same speed relative to them, regardless of their own state of motion, either toward or away from the source of light they were observing. ...Einstein opted to assume that Maxwell's theory was fundamental and not observer-dependent."

Lawrence M. Krauss, *The Edge of Knowledge: Unsolved Mysteries of the Cosmos* (2023) (Kindle), loc.188-92.

When examining the Twins' Paradox (one twin stays on Earth while the other travels at close to the speed of light many light years away, then turns around and returns), we concluded that during the trip, each twin observed that time passed more slowly for the other twin (since each appeared to the other to be moving away at close to the speed of light), yet when reunited, it turns out that the traveling twin has aged much less than the stay-at-home twin. We concluded that the explanation is that the aging (time) differences arose during the initial acceleration of the spacecraft and the deceleration and acceleration to turn around and the deceleration to land. Those movements were not relative, but "real."

As for gravity, empirical evidence shows that time slows down when gravity increases. As a matter of theory, as an object approaches a Black Hole, it would appear to an observer that time for the object continues to slow until the object reaches the Black Hole's event horizon at which point time will appear to stop. Thus, the observer would never see the object enter the Black Hole. Of course, the object passes right through the event horizon into the Black Hole.

"[C]onsider a person falling in toward the event horizon of a large black hole and emitting an SOS signal by waving a flashlight at some regular rate. As they approach the event horizon, the time between the flashes you might see will get longer. You can think of this as the ticking of a clock that gets slower and slower. But more than that, the wavelength of the radiation in each flash will also get longer as the waves get stretched out, rising up out of the potential well. The light in each flash will go from blue, say, to yellow, to orange, to red—and after that to infrared, to microwaves, and to radio waves. ...In their own timeframe they would cross the event horizon without noticing anything strange. But for an outside observer, they would appear to freeze just outside the event horizon. ...[A]n outside observer won't actually see this freezing, because the light from the infalling victim's flashlight will be redshifted to ever longer wavelengths until it is literally undetectable. The person will thus disappear from view before they actually cross the event horizon."

Krauss, *The Edge of Knowledge,* loc.342-55.

The twins would physically age differently. So, time must be more than an illusion or human phenomenon.

Or, look at GPS:

"If you have ever used the GPS on your phone to guide you as you drive or walk, you have relied on the fact that we know about gravitational redshift and can adjust our atomic clocks accordingly. ...[D]ue to the effects of special relativity, the speed of the satellites slows their tick rate by about seven microseconds each day, while due to general relativity, their higher altitude causes their tick rate to speed up by about forty-five microseconds each day."

Id., loc.287.

These are real physical differences in our world; but, still, maybe time emerges only at a macro level.

CHAPTER 4

Fine-Tuning

"The anthropic principle
is a counsel of despair....
a negation of our hopes of understanding
the underlying order of the universe,
on the basis of science."

Stephan Hawking
Quoted by Thomas Hertog

In 1998, Thomas Hertog, a beginning graduate student in Cambridge's renowned Department of Applied Mathematics and Theoretical Physics, began to work under the guidance of Stephan Hawking. The collaboration grew and was to last 20 years until Hawking's death in 2018. Hertog provides quite interesting, if a bit glamorized, descriptions of how Hawking managed to continue his work almost to the end. *On the Origin of Time: Stephen Hawking's Final Theory* (2023). Here, however, I am focused on the science.

The book includes a lot of theoretical physics as background and for context, which is original and very insightful. I hope that I have captured the essence of Hawking's thoughts in this greatly abbreviated description.

As I have described, many twentieth century physicists (and other scientists) were resistant to the Big Bang theory because it contemplated a beginning, a creation. Hertog quotes Einstein, Eddington and others expressing such concerns. The problem was not just the resemblance to the book of *Genesis*. If the beginning occurred in a "singularity," then our theories of physics could offer no explanation of what happened because they breakdown inside a Black Hole or singularity. If time began with the Big Bang, then we can expect no explanations consistent with our understanding of causality where a cause precedes the effect in time (nothing preceded in time, because there was no time). Now, these were not scientific problems as such, but matters of public perception.

DESIGN

The concerns were greatly exasperated by the increasing awareness of "fine-tuning" problem (that the Universe was exceptionally well adjusted to sustain life, especially complex life like humans). Traditional physics was based on a model of explanation in which the observed "initial conditions" and the discovered "Laws of Nature" predicted the outcome. In such a framework, the future complexity of the outcome will have been somehow embedded in the initial conditions.

So, the staggeringly unlikely relationships necessary for life to exist would have been contained in the initial conditions existing at the beginning, conditions for which we have no scientific explanation.

"[I]t appears as if the universe has somehow been designed to make life possible. ...[T]he judicious tunings that render it habitable at all are by no means superficial qualities of the world. Instead they are inscribed deeply in the mathematical form of the laws of physics. ...So the riddle of design in cosmology is that the fundamental laws of physics appear to be specifically engineered to facilitate the emergence of life."

Id., pp.8, 9.

Or, in words that are attributed by Hertog to Hawking:

"[T]he universe we observe appears designed... .
[A]lmost as if the geneses of life and the cosmos
are entwined with each other,
that the cosmos knew all along
that one day it would be our home."

...

"What are we to make of
this mysterious appearance of intent?"

Id., pp.xiii-xv.

Just coincidence? Perhaps. If we say that the future was not specified at the beginning, it makes little sense to describe the outcome as highly improbable. As I discussed in *Important Things*, every complicated series of events that actually occurs would be characterizable as "highly improbable" in advance. Perhaps, then, the discomfort is simply from "our failure to appreciate how many opportunities there are for coincidences to occur. When we are allowed to identify them *post hoc*, coincidences are not unlikely at all; they're pretty much guaranteed to happen." Steven Pinker, *Rationality: What It Is, Why It Seems Scarce, Why It Matters* (2021), p.143.

But, all of this?

Hertog enumerates many of the more striking bio-enabling features of the Universe:

- three dimensional space;

- the temporary (8 billion year) pause in the rate of expansion of the Universe to allow the formation of aggregations of matter, including galaxies (in 1998, it was discovered that the expansion of the Universe began accelerating again about 5 billion years ago);

- the properties of the elementary particles and forces; just the right-sized tiny variations in the temperature of the Big Bang residual radiation;

- the balance in strengths between the strong nuclear force and the electromagnetic force for the synthesis of carbon from helium in stars;

- the small size of the Higgs boson;

- the very low entropy of the beginning point and

- dark energy ("The value of the dark energy density that we've measured is extraordinarily small.... . Yet this smallness is precisely what made the universe 'hesitate' for about eight billion years before dark energy was able to muster sufficient strength to accelerate the expansion").

Id., pp.6-9.

Astro-physicist Lawrence Krauss seeks to dismiss the fine-tuning problem, asserting:

"[Darwin and Wallace] demonstrated that the earth wasn't fine-tuned to fit life, but that only life that was fine-tuned (by evolution) to fit the earth would survive. I emphasize this point because for some reason the same debate has surfaced again, but this time in cosmology. The point is stressed over and over again by people who believe that there must have been an intelligent creator for our universe, that if any one of a number of fundamental constants took values that were even slightly different than their actual values, life as we know it could never have evolved. The point is that the universe isn't fine-tuned for life. Rather, life on earth arose because it could. Just as in the case of biological evolution, life is fine-tuned for the universe, rather than the other way around."

Lawrence M. Krauss, *The Edge of Knowledge: Unsolved Mysteries of the Cosmos* (2023) (Kindle), loc.2573-85.

Rather clever. It gives one a moment's pause. But, just a moment's. Unless life is possible in a very wide range of forms and environments (which Krauss argues is a possibility and tries various arguments in an attempt to explain why we have no evidence of it if that is true), then it makes no sense to suggest that life "evolved" to fit the conditions existing. We are back to fine tuning.

The trendy solution to this unpalatable state of affairs is the "multiverse" coupled with the "Anthropic Principle." The hypothesis of many, perhaps an infinite number of, universes gained support from M–theory, a sort of meta-theory embracing all of the five (or six) existing versions of string theory. With an infinite number of universes, every possible version would exist, including ours. Simple logic tells us that we must be in a bio-friendly version, since we exist. Actually, with an infinite number of universes, we must be in at least one of the infinite number of bio-friendly universes that would exist. There is part of the problem.

This solution has foresworn all predictive power. It explains nothing, because it is compatible with everything. As to our Universe, we have no answers; other universes with which we have not had, and never can have, any contact or information exchange cannot be the "cause" of any aspect of our existence.

So, like Hawking, we abandon the Anthropic Multiverse as an answer.

AN ALTERNATIVE?

It appears that during his collaboration with Hertog, Hawking concluded that he had gotten it wrong in his best-selling book *A Brief History of Time*. I made substantial use of that book in *Important Things*, but not without expressing some reservations. (In fact, in the essay called "Turn, Turn, Turn," I expressed a different view of time.)

However, in 2010, Hawking, with Leonard Mlodinow, published *The Grand Design* (which I criticize in *Important Things*), endorsing M-theory and predicting the imminent realization of a Theory of Everything. Hertog suggests that Hawking was in the process of largely rejecting those views at the time. "Midway through our collaboration he wrote a book, *The Grand Design*, which reflects our confusion at the time. In it Stephen clings to the anthropic principle, the multiverse, and the idea of a final theory of everything, down to its rivalry with a God-created universe." *Id.*, p.xx.

Hawking apparently was reexamining the fundamental assumptions of theoretical physics, in some part as a response to thinking about Darwin's theory of evolution. If we set aside determinism, the need for prediction, the falsifiability test; if we assume that the Laws of Nature can change; if we allow a role for chance, for accidents; then we can examine where we are and how we got there. A top-down, rather than the traditional bottom-up, approach. More like biology or history than physics.

Then, we may be able to investigate layer by layer, backwards in time, and identity what changed from stage to stage. We are likely to find that the Laws evolved (changed) over time. We may realize that the future evolution of the Universe (although, physicists use it, I do not like to use the word "evolution" in this context because it suggests the Darwinian concept when all it should really mean is the process of change) was not contained in the initial conditions, but was the result of chance events along the way, that it could have turned out very differently. In other words, that the initial conditions and Laws were not determinative.

> "The chance outcomes at countless branching events in-fuse a genuinely emergent element into evolution. They add a vast amount of structure and information that simply isn't contained in the lower-level laws, out of which new law-like patterns at higher levels can—and often do—emerge."

Id., p.21. *See also, id.*, p.189.

This idea was not new. It was expressed by the Belgian priest/astronomer Georges Lemaître in an iconic paper published in *Nature* in May 1931: "The Beginning of the World from the Point of View of Quantum Theory."

As Hertog explains:

"Lemaître's cosmopoetic letter is one of the most audacious scientific texts of the twentieth century. It counts no more than 457 words but can be regarded as the charter of big bang cosmology. In this letter he argues, to my knowledge for the first time, that the relativity and quantum revolutions are profoundly interconnected, that the beginning of the universe should be part of science, governed by physical laws that we can discover, but that these hypothetical laws will involve a mixture of quantum theory with gravity."

...

"Lemaître ended his letter in Nature by saying: 'Clearly the initial quantum could not conceal in itself the whole course of evolution. The story of the world need not have been written down in the first quantum like the song on a disc of a phonograph....Instead from the same beginning widely different universes could have evolved.'

...

"Could it be that causality fades away in a quantum origin, that the mystery of the 'first cause' evaporates in a quantum world—our world?"

Id., pp.61, 62.

We know that quantum mechanics introduced uncertainty, indeterminacy, into physics and that relativity and quantum theories have been highly resistant to reconciliation. We also know that quantum fluctuations occur spontaneously and randomly. So, a different approach is certainly worth exploring. Does the top-down approach solve our problem?

Of course, such an explanation is, by definition, not predictive, and it is not subject to the Popperian falsifiability standard. (But, does it provide insight, even understanding?) As I discussed in *Important Things*, and as Hertog points out, the same things are true of the theory of natural selection (and all Darwinian theories); yet, they are deemed science. They provide explanations and insights, what we might call "knowledge." But, natural selection has something more than randomness. It has a mechanism for selection, an explanation for the direction of evolution. What about our top-down cosmology?

Here, we need to add in more quantum theory.

Based on a variety of two-slit experiments and the Heisenberg Uncertainty Principle, quantum theorists concluded that every particle will follow many different paths until the moment it is observed, at which point its path becomes determined. Bohr theorized that upon observation, the wave function representing the particle "collapses" into one path In the alternative construction, Schrödinger's equation, however, wave functions do not collapse—they smoothly fluctuate. Nonetheless, a single path for a wave is specified or established upon observation. (How?)

"[T]he waves the Schrödinger equation speaks of aren't physical waves. Schrödinger did not say that particles are somehow smeared out over space. The waves of quantum mechanics are a bit more abstract, they are more like 'waves of probability' that describe different possible positions of pointlike particles." *Id.*, p.87.

One difference between these theoretical constructions is that in Bohr's version, the multiple paths would be lost upon collapse, whereas under the Schrödinger equation, the wave functions would remain as part of the Universe's history. Hertog and, presumably, Hawking concluded that Schrödinger's formulation was closer to reality.

Hawking decided that he and other physicists had erred in approaching the cosmological questions from the perspective of an omnipotent outside observer. Instead, we are part of the Universe we are trying to explain (similar to Einstein's conclusion that there is no absolute space nor absolute time). So, we need a theory that incorporates the initial conditions, the Laws of Nature and the observer to replace the traditional dualism. Hawking postulates that we as observers—and through our acts of observation, as we examine the past—determine our history of the Universe. Thus, the circumstances of the Universe did not just happen any which way, but evolved so that we exist, because our history necessarily includes us.

> "Observership draws the past more firmly into existence, but it doesn't transmit information back in time. ...Quantum cosmology doesn't deny that the past has happened; rather it refines what it means 'to happen' and, especially, what can— and what cannot—be said about the past."

Id., p.196.

"...[O]bservership in quantum cosmology [is] an agency operating at a deeper level, an indispensable part of the continual process through which physical reality ... comes about. ...One doesn't follow the universe from the bottom up—forward in time—because one no longer presumes the universe has an objective observer-independent history, with a definite starting point... . [H]istory at the very deepest level emerges backward in time."

Id., p.188.

"The theory traces the fitness for life ultimately to the fact that deep down at the quantum level, a tangible universe and observership are tied together. The anthropic principle is rendered obsolete... .

...

"Observership in quantum cosmology ... encapsulates the more fundamental quantum act of observation... : the process whereby at branching points in history one particular result from a range of possible results is converted into a fact."

...

"We create the universe as much as the universe creates us."

Id., pp.198, 187, 209.

Asking the question "what happened?" apparently itself "retroactively draws into existence those few branches of cosmological history that have the properties that are being observed." *Id.*, p.188. One might imagine a multitude of possible histories stored in the "memory" of the Universe, awaiting an observer. Observation then establishes the position of a particle, which determines its future path as well as its past. The edifice of endless possibilities crumbles, leaving a particular past or history in place. But, who makes the crucial observation(s)?

Who is his "observer"? Humanity as a whole? Or, is there a distinct history for each of us who asks the question? Or, something else? Hertog suggests that it need not be a human being, or even a conscious being: "Top-down cosmology retrodicts that **the observation performed by the most primitive environment** in the earliest stages of expansion that three dimensions broke loose and began to inflate carves out those few histories among all possible ones that end up with three large dimensions." *Id.*, p.199 (emphasis added).

Thus, the observations fixing the history already happened, so we appear to face a previously established Universe, not one waiting for us to ask the question. If so, then what is the role of the current observer? Of us?

Where are we then?

Ahead?

I think not by much.

I previously wrote the following about a theory propounded by Lee Smolin:

> "Smolin outlines the type of new theory that he envisages. First, the Laws of Nature are not timeless and unchanging. They change and evolve over time. Second, the process is central. Using a Darwinian model, Smolin suggests that there has been a series of universes created, and they have had different laws governing them. The universes with laws that favor the creation of new universes eventually come to dominate the set of all universes. Our Universe, he explains, has Laws that favor the creation of new universes and, therefore, not surprisingly, is readily available to be the one in which we find ourselves. *Time Reborn* [2013], pp.123–39. **His Darwinian model, however, is lacking the necessary element—the survival pressure—that makes the process work."**

Important Things, p.326 (emphasis added).

This "new" theory has similar deficiencies. I have a lot of sympathy for the abandonment of determinism and the related dualistic explanatory paradigm. But, I am less enamored with quantum theory based incorporation of observership. I think that a theory that includes the observers is desirable, even necessary, but I find that that presented by Hertog to be unsatisfying.

"TIME WITHOUT TIME"

The penultimate chapter, entitled "Time without time", describes Hawking's strong interest, during his final years, in holography. Hertog declares that, "[t]he theoretical discovery of holography ranks among the most important and far-reaching discoveries in physics of the late twentieth century." *Id.*, p.213.

Why? We need some more history.

In 1974, Hawking announced that black holes radiated heat, contrary to their characterization as utterly cold and dark (black). His calculations showed that the radiation from black holes had the exact same characteristics as so-called "thermal black-body radiation," which had provoked Planck's proposal of quanta, beginning the development of quantum mechanics. Hawking went on to calculate the temperature of black holes, producing the formula displayed on the medallion created to memorialize his internment at Westminster Abbey in 2018.

"The letter M in this formula stands for the mass of the black hole. The remaining quantities are all basic constants of nature: c is the speed of light, G is Newton's gravitational constant, ℏ is Planck's quantum constant, and k is Boltzmann's constant for thermodynamics—the study of energy, heat, and work. The sheer beauty of Hawking's formula is that it brings together all these constants in a single equation."

Id., p. 214.

From this formula for temperature, Hawking derived the formula for the entropy of black holes.

"Roughly speaking, higher entropy means that more information can be stored in a system's microscopic details without changing its overall macroscopic properties. ...As a matter of fact, Hawking wasn't the first to propound that black holes have entropy. ...[In 1972,] ...physicist Jacob Bekenstein had advanced the idea that black holes possess an entropy in proportion to the area, A, of their horizon surface. At the time nearly everyone in the scientific community—Stephen up front!—dismissed Bekenstein's idea because, well, black holes don't radiate and hence they can't have entropy. With his discovery of Hawking radiation, Stephen inadvertently proved Bekenstein right. Bekenstein and Hawking's entropy formula predicts that black holes have a truly gigantic information storage capacity."

Id., pp.215-6.

But, there is a further implication, which is that the information storage capacity is determined by the surface area, not the volume, of the black hole.

So, now the problem is that as the black hole radiates, it slowly shrinks until it disappears—it effectively evaporates. What happens to the information that it had stored? Quantum theory says that information cannot be lost, so it cannot just disappear (unless quantum mechanics is wrong).

For the answer, we enter the realm of pure speculation.

In 1997, Juan Maldacena, an assistant professor at Harvard, proposed a theory based upon a supposed duality linking a string theory with gravity and a particle theory (quantum field theory) without gravity. The particle theory exists in one less dimension than the string theory (three rather than four). Maldacena asserted that these two theories were equivalent. If so, then in a bounded world (like a black hole), the quantum fields and particles on the surface of the boundary, without any gravity, would reflect precisely the behavior of the matter with gravity inside the boundary. Thus, the hologram. This supposed holographic dualism means that all of the information inside the black hole also resides on the surface, in one less dimension.somewhere.

Then, it is suggested, the information manages to escape along with the Hawking radiation, to reappear (perhaps, in a different spacetime). We do not know how the information is stored inside the black hole, how it is translated in the transfer to the the surface, how it is transferred to the surface, how it then escapes or where it goes. We also are unable to read or access it inside the black hole, on the surface (the hologram) or wherever it ends up.

Yet,

> "the holographic duality states that **a boundary world of quantum fields and particles fully specifies the behavior of gravity and matter** inside..., and not just a classical or semiclassical approximation of it. ...Hence holography—in its ambitious form—provides **a working example of a complete quantum theory of gravity and matter**. ...[R]elativity and quantum theory aren't antagonists but merely alternative vantage points on the same physical reality."

Id., pp.225-6 (emphasis added).

"...Physical systems can be gravitational and quantum at the same time, holography says, albeit in different dimensions." *Id.*

Great.

But, what does all have to do with time? Ah, more fantasy.

Our expanding Universe appears to have no boundaries, unlike black holes. However, Hawking recast the Universe in imaginary time. Then,"[t]he no-boundary origin of the universe lies at the center of the disk, where time has morphed into space. The universe today corresponds to the circular boundary. [This results from] a hypersphere, namely the three-dimensional surface in four-dimensional spacetime to which all our observations of the universe are roughly confined." *Id.*, p.239. The crowded outer edge (surface of the hypersphere) is considered the boundary in which the hologram resides. (This supposed surface consists of everything in the Universe as of the particular time being considered. Rather like one "slice" of Julian Barbour's spacetime.)

> "The chief difference between holograms that mirror [black hole] interiors and those of inflating universes lies in the nature of the extra dimension that pops out. In the former case the emergent direction is a curved dimension of space. It is the interior depth [of the black hole]. In the case of an expanding universe, the time dimension is emergent. That is, history itself is holographically encrypted."

Id., p.241.

"Holography envisions that physical reality isn't just made up of real things, like particles of matter and radiation or even the field of spacetime, but that it takes a far more abstract entity as well: quantum information." *Id.*, p.244.

"According to classical general relativity, black holes are the epitome of simplicity. In the end, it is fully characterized by just two numbers: its total mass and angular momentum. But Bekenstein and Hawking's semiclassical entropy formula paints a very different picture. It portrays black holes as the most complicated objects in nature, the exact opposite of their classical image."

Id., p.216.

ORIGIN?

Oh, yes, the origin of time.

"I [Hawking] have changed my mind. [A] *Brief History* [of Time] is written from the wrong perspective.

...

"You took a God's-eye perspective on the universe in *A Brief History*, I propounded, as if we are somehow looking at the universe or its wave function from outside of it."

...

"So did Newton and Einstein, he said, as if in defense."

Hertog, pp.165-6.

Hertog says that Hawking later wrote: "[W]e should think of **the universe as a superposition of many possible spacetimes. So a quantum universe is uncertain even on the very largest scales... .**" *Id.*, p.174 (emphasis added).

So, we have "a completely different and profoundly counterintuitive way of looking at reality, in which the expansion of space—and indeed time itself—is a manifestly emergent phenomenon, stitched out of a myriad of quantum threads forming a timeless world lying in a lower-dimensional surface." *Id.*, p.248.

"The no-boundary hypothesis predicts that if we trace the primordial universe as far back in time as we possibly can, its structural properties continue to evaporate and transmute and that this extends, ultimately, to time itself. Time would initially have been melded with space into something like a higher-dimensional sphere, closing the universe into nothingness. This led the early Hawking ... to proclaim that the universe was created from nothing. But Hawking's final theory offers a radically different interpretation of this closure of spacetime at the big bang. The later Hawking held that this nothingness at the beginning is nothing like the emptiness of a vacuum, out of which universes may or may not be born, but **a much more profound, epistemic horizon involving no space, no time, and, crucially, no physical laws.**"

Id., pp.256-7 (emphasis added).

Thus,"[I]n a holographic universe, time would, in a sense, be illusory." *Id.*, p.242. "[H]olography places **the true origin of the universe in the distant future,** because only the far future would reveal the hologram in its full glory." *Id.*, p.245 (emphasis added).

So...?

Hell if I know.

Postscript

I think there is more to be said about the role of the observer. I do not mean "observer" in the sense of quantum theory, but in the sense of conscious awareness. Perception, experience, response. Twentieth century physics tells us, based upon Relativity, that a solitary object has no location and no velocity. It is only with the presence of some other object that position and velocity are able to be established. (Acceleration, however, can be detected for a solitary thing. Curious?) "If space contained but a single entity the entity would not be there. There would be nothing there for it to be there to." Cormac McCarthy, *Stella Maris* (2022), p.38.

In an important sense, neither the color red nor a rainbow exist without someone to see it. Absent an observer, either is only reflected or absorbed (or, for the rainbow, deflected) frequencies of light. The same is true for the sound of "lapping" waves. Just vibrations. But, for conscious, sentient beings, these phenomena are much, much more. Indeed, "it could be true that the Earth is the only place where sensations of colour exist. Or sensations of anything: sweetness, warmth, bitterness, pain." Nicholas Humphrey, *Sentience: The Invention of Consciousness* (2023), p.86.

"There were no starry skies
prior to the first sentient and ocular being
to behold them.
Before that all was blackness and silence.

"And yet it moved.

"And yet."

Cormac McCarthy, *The Passenger* (2022), p.149 (emphasis added).

"*E pur si muove* (And yet it moves), so the story goes, is what Galileo mumbled when leaving the Inquisition that had found him guilty of heresy, forced him to abjure his Copernican views, and put him under arrest for life." Giulio Tononi, *Phi: A Voyage from the Brain to the Soul* (2012), p.36.

"It was hard to avoid the sense that the visual world is the creation of beings with the eyes to do so. Not created out of nothing **but out of that something whose actual reality is forever unknowable....**And the question once again of the nature of that reality to which there was no witness. All of this **until the first living creature possessed of vision agreed to imprint the universe upon its primitive and trembling sensorium and then to touch it with color and movement and memory.**"

McCarthy, *Stella Maris*, p.40 (emphasis added).

"'If a tree falls in the forest, does it make a sound if no one is around to hear it?' Indeed, there is no sound without a conscious observer to hear. Furthermore, there isn't even a tree or a forest, as these concepts depend on a conscious subject discerning a tree from other trees, treating them as different from the soil they are planted in or from the air that surrounds them. Nature knows nothing of these distinctions, of trees and forests, but only of formless stuff. Without a conscious subject, there are only 'atoms and the void... .'"

Christof Koch, *Then I Am Myself the World: What Consciousness Is and How to Expand It* (2024), p.103.

Perhaps, in the absence of an observer, all that there is is a sputtering, simmering "soup" of energy and fields, with particles popping in and out of existence and quantum fluctuations. Perhaps, the "macro" characteristics of the Universe appear only when observed. If so, then our act of conscious observation creates the world we see.

CHAPTER 5

Imagining

As we know, the theories of Newtonian physics do not include time. It is an external factor. When the passage of time is added to the mix, we get motion (change) and can calculate velocities. With Einstein's General Theory of Relativity, time becomes part of the theory, but it is merely the fourth dimension of spacetime.

I previously wrote:

"The concept of spacetime eliminates time as we know it. It suggests that any point in time (and space) is simply a location in an already existing structure. *See* Tegmark, *Our Mathematical Universe: My Quest for the Ultimate Nature of Reality* (2014), p.272. So, Einstein's General Theory of Relativity, unlike Newtonian mechanics, does expressly incorporate time. But, time, like the other dimensions, is reversible. Just as one can move up and down and back and forth, one can move into the past and into the future."

Important Things We Don't Know, p.323.

In quantum mechanics, time just disappears. It has no role and no meaning. Indeed, not just time but also cause and effect, past and future, even change.

> "Julian Barbour ... has argued that the Universe consists of an infinite series of slices or snap-shots or frozen moments, all of which exist now and always. Each slice contains everything that exists at the particular instance that the slice represents... . *See, e.g.*, Barbour, *The End of Time*, pp.35–57. **We experience individual slices at various moments, but all of the slices exist simultaneously. Thus, there is no real change that ever occurs**, only the appearance (or illusion) of change as we perceive different slices."

Id., p.324 (emphasis added).

Thus, there is no:

> "...difference between the past and the future. Nowhere in the laws of physics are there labels on different moments of time to indicate 'has happened yet' and 'has not happened yet.' Those laws refer equally well to any moment in time, and they tie all of the moments together in a unique order."

Sean M. Carroll, *The Big Picture: On the Origins of Life, Meaning, and the Universe Itself* (2016), p.60.

We cannot see the future but think that we remember the past. That asymmetry is the source of our perception of time and its passage.

"The future may be predicted, but it cannot be remembered. This imbalance accords quite well with our intuitive feeling that the past and the future have very different ontological statuses; one has happened, the other hasn't. ...[A]memory isn't some kind of direct access to events in the past. It must be a feature of the present state, since the present state is all we presently have. And yet there is an epistemic asymmetry, an imbalance of knowledge, between past and future."

Carroll, *The Big Picture*, p.61.

So, we speculate that time may be an emergent property that requires the presence of consciousness to arise. And, yet, onsciousness is an emergent property that requires the presence of time?

Is it possible that our minds were formed to create an awareness of time? Could there be intelligent beings with a different perception?

Let's start imagining.

Science fiction short story writer Ted Chiang presents an encounter between humans and quite different alien beings in "Story of Your Life," *Arrival* (2016) (originally published as *Stories of Your Life and Others* (2002)), pp.89–141.

The aliens ("heptapods") saw and experienced things simultaneously, not sequentially.

Louise, the narrator, observes:

"When the ancestors of humans and heptapods first acquired the spark of consciousness, they both perceived the same physical world, but they parsed their perceptions differently... . Humans had developed a sequential mode of awareness, while heptapods had developed a simultaneous mode of awareness. We experienced events in an order, and perceived their relationship as cause and effect. They experienced all events at once, and perceived a purpose underlying them all."

Chiang, *Arrival*, p.130.

The heptapods live in Sean Carroll's world (discussed in another essay). Their present contains the past and the future. There is no causation (something may have caused the Universe to be as it is, but that would be external to this model of reality). So, we have the determinist's dream.

What about free will?

Louise claims:

"Freedom isn't an illusion; it's perfectly real in the context of sequential consciousness."

...

"Within the context of simultaneous consciousness, freedom is not meaningful, but neither is coercion; it's simply a different context, no more or less valid than the other."

...

"[K]nowledge of the future was incompatible with free will. What made it possible for me to exercise freedom of choice also made it impossible for me to know the future."

Id., p.133.

So, in our dimension, people actually have choices and make decisions. Or, at least, they think they do. But, do these decisions affect the world in the future? We certainly think that they will, playing out different possible scenarios in our heads, assessing the various likely outcomes or consequences. We also clearly believe that they did, feeling relief, joy, puzzlement or guilt about the outcome and our presumed role in bringing it about. Indeed, a major source of stress is the perceived need to make decisions.

"It has now been clearly established that decision-making (and I would like to remove every trace of conscious connotation from the word 'decision') is precisely what stress is." Julian Jaynes, *The Origin of Consciousness in the Breakdown of the Bicameral Mind* (1976, 1990) (2000 edition), p.93.

So, how can the past and future all be contained in the present?

We return to the notion of multiple alternative histories, all existing simultaneously, with one to be perceived by us when we observe the past. The heptapods presumably would "see" all of the possible histories and make sense of the panoply of alternative events.

Thus, we may conclude that time is an emergent phenomenon brought into being by conscious minds and the past and present are emergent phenomena brought into being by inquiring minds.

The future? It is there in multiple versions, waiting for future observers.

And, that's the way the world would be,
if we were heptapods.

Causation

CHAPTER 6

Scientific Incompleteness and Causal Emergence

There are two interesting concepts Erik Hoel discusses on which I would like to comment: scientific incompleteness and causal emergence. *See* Erik Hoel, *The World Behind the World: Consciousness, Free Will, and the Limits of Science* (2023).

SCIENTIFIC INCOMPLETENESS

In *Important Things,* I discussed the debates over whether there were limits to what science could explain, whether due to limitations of the human mind or to oddities of reality itself. I noted that Bertrand Russell had concluded that mathematics logically could not be set forth as a complete and consistent set. I described some of the implications of Gödel's proof that physics was necessarily indeterminate. And, I mentioned Roger Penrose's argument that the mind was more than a calculator, that it was non-algorithmic.

"[S]cience's queen, mathematics, ... has been on epistemically shaky grounds ever since Bertrand Russell wondered: 'Does the set of all sets that don't contain themselves contain itself'? If the set does contain itself, it shouldn't contain itself. If the set doesn't contain itself, it should. It's un-defined. And this was the beginning of the collapse of certainty that ended in Gödel's theorems showing that formal systems built on axioms were necessarily incomplete and, not only that, that they could not prove their own consistency. It showed that there are doors mathematics cannot open, that there are walls it cannot climb, that it is hemmed in by an invisible force that one cannot see but only deduce."

...

"Similarly, there is the argument in Roger Penrose's *The Emperor's New Mind,* another classic book, that the human mind is non-algorithmic. This is a decades-old argument—Penrose gives by far the best and clearest version of it but it goes back to the 1960s, originally proposed by philosopher J. R. Lucas."

Hoel, *The World Behind the World,* pp.145, 152.

Anything else? We have noted that science has been based on an extrinsic perspective, the observer is outside of the phenomena being studied and have discussed (especially, in this volume) how that methodology may be insufficient.

"[S]uch an omniscient viewpoint appears to be incomplete. It is missing information. ...For isn't someone conceiving of this 'view from nowhere'? The conceiver has a unique perspective, but under the most extrinsic of perspectives there are no unique perspectives, indeed there are explicitly no perspectives at all."

Id., pp.144, 145.

Yet, if the observer becomes part of the theory, we may encounter the self-referral or infinite recursiveness problems that plague other logical systems."[W]e should ask if science itself has similar limits to its knowledge. Not limitations due to complexity, or difficulty, but rather based on fundamental foundational constraints." *Id.*, p.145.

> "[W]e can imagine that science could be said to be complete if all questions about scientific theories can be answered, or, equivalently, if all statements made in some sort of hypothetical 'language of science' can be decided as true or false (versus some being undecidable). Perhaps science too contains the strange loop of self-reference, fatal flaws, holes where knowledge should be. Let us call this idea 'scientific incompleteness.' ...Wouldn't we expect to find difficulties in science precisely around observers, if the paradoxes that self-reference engenders in mathematics are kept in mind?"

Id., pp.144-5.

"A Gödel sentence claims about itself that 'this sentence is not provable in S wherein S is some formal system. It is basically a complexified version of the liar's paradox ('I am lying to you right now'). If the liar's claim is true, then it's false, and if it's false, then it's true. ...The Lucas-Penrose argument is that some form of this proof means that the human mind is not a machine, since we can 'see' the truth of the Gödel sentence, even if S cannot. ...[W]e ourselves would know that the sentence is true, but meanwhile the formal description cannot know this—and therefore, the formal system S (like a brain emulation on a computer) is not really a full mimic of our mind, no matter how perfectly copied. It is an incomplete simulacrum."

Id., pp.152-3.

"[S]cientific incompleteness has nothing to do with the limits of intelligence, nor the conceptual or sensory apparatuses that a certain species is equipped with. It is about reality itself containing innately undecideable properties, often triggered by paradoxical self-recursion of knowledge." *Id.*, p.157.

"[T]he physicist Lawrence Krauss wrote an entire book called *A Universe from Nothing*, and yet what he really put forward was a speculative account of how the universe of matter could arise from 'merely' an unstable vacuum and the laws of physics." *Id.*, p.149.

CAUSAL EMERGENCE

I have previously discussed causation. Many of us believe that identifying causes is an important goal of science. Many probably think explaining causation is too. But, what is causation? Following David Hume, we might say, if B always follows A, then A causes B; yet, that relationship is only correlation. If B only occurs following A, we are closer.

So, Hoel describes the "intervention" test. ("Judea Pearl, research for which he was given the Turing Award... . Pearl formalized the idea of an intervention as key to analyzing causation. An intervention is when an experimenter manipulates a variable in a system.") If an observer intervenes and removes A from the experiment, does B not appear? If so, then we have found a cause of B. Now consider different scales (or levels, as Carroll refers to it). At the microscale, there may be several or, even, very many configurations of the elements that are consistent with a particular macroscale characteristic, for example, where the macro characteristic is a statistical result of a large number of micro elements. Further suppose that the elimination of that macro characteristic results in the disappearance of something. We would say that that macro characteristic was a cause of that something. But, what intervention at the microscale could result in the absence of that macroscale something? Hoel would say that we discovered causal emergence at that particular macroscale.

"When I refer to causation, this is to what I refer: the influence of one variable in a model on another, which we can separate out from correlation by performing interventions. And as Pearl points out, once we have a causal model, we can conceptualize not just actual performable interventions, but hypothetical or imaginable ones—that is, we can reason counterfactually."

Id., p.175.

So, what has happened? Hoel says that the phenomenon is "a middle ground" between weak and strong emergence.

"[O]ntological (or strong) emergence and epistemic (or weak) emergence. ...Ontological emergence, in the sense that matters here, concerns the emergence of genuinely novel properties at some non-fundamental level, while epistemic emergence concerns the emergence of greater explanatory or predictive power at some higher level of description, relative to our epistemic capacities."

Joe Dewhurst, "Causal Emergence and Real Patterns," *philsci-archive.pitt.edu*, April 3, 2020.

So, does the macroscale simply reveal an explanation of the cause or has something more been added to the picture? We clearly may feel that our understanding has been increased, but have we fundamentally learned anything? The macroscale might eliminate the chaos or disorder at the microscale or just make it easier for us to see the patterns disguised by the noise. "[T]here being greater 'power' in the causal relationships at higher levels of description—not that anything ontologically novel has emerged, but rather that this level of description gives us a better grip on the 'real' causal dynamics of the system. Perhaps this is in fact all there is to causation... ." *Id*.

The critic says:

> "[O]ur interventions will more reliably bring about the state that we are interested in... . It is only in this interventionist sense that there is 'more' causation in the macroscale system than in its microscale equivalent, because we are able to more reliably predict the outcome of an arbitrary intervention. ...[But,] interven[ing] at the macro-level ... **will necessarily also involve a micro-level intervention.** So even if we can intervene more reliably (at least relative to macro-level outcomes) by targeting the macro-level, it doesn't seem like there are really any novel causal processes taking place at this level, because **corresponding causal processes will always be taking place at the micro-level.**"

Id. (emphasis added).

Is that right?

"Causal emergence occurs when macroscales have more causal influence than their underlying microscales over the exact same events. ...[T]he macroscale is a cause while the microscale is not. The more error correction there is at a macroscale, the stronger the causal influence will be in comparison to the underlying microscale, and therefore the greater degree of causal emergence there will be. ...Causal emergence ... holds that the elements and states of macroscales are reducible to underlying microscales without loss, but that the causation of the macroscale is not."

Hoel, *The World Behind the World*, pp.177, 188, 189.

CHAPTER 7

Phase Transitions and Superconductors

As water approaches its boiling (or freezing) point, there is no indication that something significant is about to happen. When that point is reached, the addition (or further removal) of heat will not change the water's temperature; although, it will hasten the completion of the transition.

Remarkable.

Many, but not all, materials experience phase transitions, especially between being a solid and being a liquid as the temperature rises (of course, the critical temperatures vary dramatically). And, there are differences in what happens.

"At a high enough temperature, glass is a liquid, but it behaves in an unusual way. If we take a container full of molten glass (or honey, or wax) and turn it upside down, the liquid does not immediately fall to the ground, but instead begins to slowly ooze from its container. ...Characteristics and interactions that, though present in glass, honey, wax, bitumen, and some metal alloys, are absent from water and almost all other liquids... ."

Giorgio Parisi, *In a Flight of Starlings: The Wonders of Complex Systems* (2023), p.64.

Importantly, the phase transitions are not the result of changes in the individual molecules, but of the relationships among them, altering the characteristics of the collective. "What we are witnessing is a collective mutation. It is not the single atom, it is not the single molecule of water that freezes or boils." *Id.*, p.45. The aggregate holds or releases latent heat (heat that is not reflected in the temperature). Characteristics like wetness, firmness, softness and conductivity arise at a macro level reflecting a sufficiently large collection of micro level elements. These characteristics are meaningless with respect to individual atoms or molecules. (This can be distinguished from characteristics that are present in the individual elements but can be detected only in a significant concentration, such as color or smell or taste.)

"[W]e have been taught to distinguish carefully between a physical change, such as melting or evaporation in which the molecules are preserved (so that, for example, alcohol, whether solid, liquid or a gas, always consists of the same molecules, C_2H_6O), and a chemical change, as, for example, the burning of alcohol, $C_2H_6O + 3O_2 = 2CO_2 + 3H_2O$, where an alcohol molecule and three oxygen molecules undergo a rearrangement to form two molecules of carbon dioxide and three molecules of water.

...

"Where we find no crystalline structure we have to regard the thing as a liquid with very high 'viscosity' (internal friction). Such a substance discloses by the absence of a well-defined melting temperature and of a latent heat of melting that it is not a true solid. When heated it softens gradually and eventually liquefies without discontinuity."

Erwin Schrödinger, "What is Life?" First published 1944.

In the early twentieth century, when physicists found experimental evidence of atoms and molecules, they tried to interpret macroscopic phenomena as emerging from the collective behavior of those small units.

So, how does it happen?

"The solution was found in the 1940s and '50s, starting from an idea that was already well known in physics: energy minimization. In nature, an object that is free to move will seek its position of lowest energy, until a point of equilibrium is reached. ...The position it has at the bottom represents a stable equilibrium position, and the ball will stay there unless something else intervenes to cause it to move again."

Parisi, *In a Flight of Starlings*, p.48.

"The actual world is disordered, and as we said at the start, many situations in the real world can be described as a large number of elementary agents that interact with each other. ...Disorder is born from the fact that certain elementary entities behave differently from others... . [D]isordered systems are simultaneously in a very high number of different states of equilibrium. ...Whenever a physical process is not in a state of equilibrium, time enters into the equation. It is always possible to distinguish a before and an after, which we can't do with systems in equilibrium."

Id., pp.80, 75, 79 (emphasis added).

Logically, we can imagine three types of relationships between the macro state and the constituent elements.

(i) Changes at the macro level might occur with no detectable changes in the individual micro level elements. That seems to be the situation with respect to water and other materials that can transform from a liquid to a solid or to a gas.

(ii) The macro-level transformation could result in ("cause") changes in the individual micro elements. Examples of this "reverse" causation have been identified by physicists.

"[W]e all agree that altering the little can change the emergent big. And the reverse certainly holds true. ...So some emergent states have downward causality... . ...Downward causation doesn't cause individual building blocks to acquire complicated skills; instead, it determines the contexts in which the blocks are doing their idiotically simple things."

Robert M. Sapolsky, *Determined: A Science of Life without Free Will* (2023), pp.198, 200.

(iii) Or, detectable changes in the individual elements might result in new characteristics at the macro level. Examples appear to be magnetism and superconductivity. However, magnetism seems to occur gradually, with the magnetic attraction becoming stronger as the percentage of constituent elements become aligned in terms of their charges; while superconductivity appears to appear and disappear suddenly (as does the material's resistance to magnetic attraction), suggesting that something significant is happening at a macro level independently from the individual elements.

Magnetism seems somewhat different from the other examples (perhaps because we understand it better). Certain materials can become magnetic when in proximity to a magnetic force that alters the alignment of individual molecules to be parallel to the applied force. The strength of the material's magnetic attraction will be proportional to the strength of the applied force, as more (or fewer) molecules become aligned. At some point, depending on temperature, the material can become magnetized, so it remains its magnetic attraction even when the applied force is removed. Apparently, this transformation is sudden, a phase change.

"[]The behavior of a magnetic system does not depend much on the behavior of the individual elementary objects of which it is composed. ... [T]he magnetization diminishing to zero in proximity to the critical temperature always follows the same trend. This trend is mathematically described by a power-law function that presents similar characteristics for a whole class of magnetic substances, including ones that are very different from each other. ...[D]espite the microscopic details being completely different, the collective behavior was the same."

Id., p.54 (emphasis added).

"The magnetization is due to the fact that the ... molecules are little magnets and tend to orientate themselves parallel to the field, like a compass needle. But you must not think that they actually all turn parallel. For if you double the field, you get double the magnetization ..., and that proportionality goes on to extremely high field strengths, the magnetization increasing at the rate of the field you apply.

...

"The orientation the field tends to produce is continually counteracted by the heat motion, which works for random orientation.

...

"If the observed weak magnetization is really the outcome of rival tendencies, namely, the magnetic field, which aims at combing all the molecules parallel, and the heat motion, which makes for random orientation, then it ought to be possible to increase the magnetization by weakening the heat motion, that is to say, by lowering the temperature... . That is confirmed by experiment, which gives the magnetization inversely proportional to the absolute temperature... ."

Schrödinger, "What is Life?"

Superconductivity

Superconductors were much in the news during the summer of 2023. (I did not much discuss electricity in *Important Things*, mainly just the electromagnetic force. So, I have added below a brief description.)

The amount of energy that is lost in the transmission of the electricity through the wire (generally as heat and light) is a result of the "resistivity" of the material of which the wire is made. The thicker the wire, the less the resistance. Also, the lower the temperature of the wire, the lower the resistance for most conducting materials. Different materials will show differences in resistivity with temperature changes. In fact, some materials like carbon experience less resistivity at high temperatures. At higher temperatures, there will tend to be more free electrons that could move; but, the atoms will tend to be bigger, creating greater chances of collisions.

"The resistivity of some materials has a strong temperature dependence. In some materials, such as copper, the resistivity increases with increasing temperature. In fact, in most conducting metals, the resistivity increases with increasing temperature. The increasing temperature causes increased vibrations of the atoms in the lattice structure of the metals, which impede the motion of the electrons. In other materials, such as carbon, the resistivity decreases with increasing temperature."

University Physics, Volume 2, "9.3 Resistivity and Resistance," *OpenStax*.

Certain materials have been found that have virtually no resistance at particular temperatures, typically very low ones. These materials are called "superconductors."

Curiously, superconductors also reject magnetic fields.

"If electrons flow in circulating currents around the surface of a superconductor, they will set up a magnetic field which is equal in magnitude but opposite in direction to the external field applied. This will cause the applied field to be completely expelled and result in the Meissner effect."

...

"Type I' superconductors have a sharp transition from the superconducting state where all magnetic flux is expelled to the normal state. Type II superconductors, on the other hand exhibit similar behaviour by completely excluding a magnetic field below a lower critical field value and becoming normal again at an upper critical field."

University of Cambridge, "Dissemination of IT for the Promotion of Materials Science." *doItpoms.ac.uk*.

Physicists now believe that they understand how superconductors "work." A theory proposed in 1957 by John Bardeen, Leon Cooper, and John Schrieffer "postulated a satisfactory explanation of the microscopic mechanism behind the effect." *Id*. It suggests that at certain temperatures and pressures electrons of opposite spin which normally repel each other can form pairs, called "Cooper pairs." The formation of these pairs reduces the chances of collisions of moving electrons. Indeed, the moving electrons encounter no resistance at all, lose no energy (produce no heat or light) and, if the superconductor material forms a closed circuit, will keep moving indefinitely without any additional energy being suppled. This basic theory of superconductivity, "BCS Theory," garnered the three scientists the 1972 Nobel Prize in physics.

"Different isotopes of the same element were found to have different critical temperatures which led scientists to consider the fact that the underlying lattice must have some contribution to the superconducting effect. It was Leon Cooper who came up with the idea that vibrations within the lattice could indeed interact with electrons and cause there to be an attraction between them."

Id.

Generally, the phases reflect and are a function of the relationships among the individual elements. A single element cannot reflect the relationships, and there will be no evidence of the relationships to be found in the individual elements. Superconductivity is different. Although, I have read different descriptions of the physical changes in the individual atoms that permits the moving electrons to do so without colliding with the atoms of the conducting material (the formation of Cooper pairs creates an energy "gap" where some electron orbits are empty; electrons move from atom to atom vibrating at the same frequency as the nuclei of the atoms), it appears that the phase transition alters certain characteristics of the atoms. Curiously, it seems that they all change at once when the critical temperature is reached. As the temperature changes further, they will all suddenly change back.

So, do we have an example of a micro-level explanation for a macro-level phase transition? Sort of, if we understood better what causes the formation of Cooper pairs. We conclude that the pairs disintegrate with the application of energy, raising the temperature of the material, and that the material stops being a superconductor only when all the pairs are gone.

The existence of a theory stimulated the search for materials that would be superconductors at more easily achieved temperatures, perhaps even room temperature. The applications would be incredibly useful. Some materials have been developed that are superconductors at temperatures well above absolute zero but far below ambient temperatures on Earth.

There have been reports of success from time to time, but none have been replicatable. Then, in the summer of 2023, great media excitement was created by a "preprint" from South Korean scientists

It read:

"For the first time in the world, we succeeded in synthesizing the room-temperature superconductor (Tc≥400 K, 127∘C) working at ambient pressure with a modified lead-apatite (LK-99) structure. ... The superconductivity of LK-99 originates from minute structural distortion by a slight volume shrinkage (0.48 %), not by external factors such as temperature and pressure. ...The unique structure of LK-99 that allows the minute distorted structure to be maintained in the interfaces is the most important factor that LK-99 maintains and exhibits superconductivity at room temperatures and ambient pressure."

Sukbae Lee, Ji-Hoon Kim, Young-Wan Kwon, "The First Room-Temperature Ambient-Pressure Superconductor," submitted 22 July 2023.

However,

"The extraordinary claim quickly grabbed the attention of the science-interested public and researchers, some of whom tried to replicate LK-99. Initial attempts did not find signs of room-temperature superconductivity, but were not conclusive. Now, after dozens of replication efforts, many specialists are confidently saying that the evidence shows LK-99 is not a room-temperature superconductor."

Dan Garisto, "LK-99 isn't a superconductor—how science sleuths solved the mystery," *Nature*, 16 August 2023.

And,

"Researchers seem to have solved the puzzle of LK-99. Scientific detective work has unearthed evidence that the material is not a superconductor, and clarified its actual properties. The conclusion dashes hopes that LK-99 — a compound of copper, lead, phosphorus and oxygen — would prove to be the first superconductor that works at room temperature and ambient pressure. Instead, studies have shown that impurities in the material — in particular, copper sulfide — were responsible... ."

Id.

"All the same, there's no reason to think room-temperature superconductivity is impossible. And if found, it could be a big deal. 'A room-temperature superconductor that was a practical engineering material would be pretty transformative,' says John Durrell, a professor of superconductor engineering at the University of Cambridge."

Philip Ball, "There's no room-temperature superconductor yet, but the quest continues," *The Guardian*, 2 September 2023.

There are reports in early 2024 that several researchers have not given up on LK-99 and are continuing to investigate it. Research is also ongoing into other candidate materials such as graphene.

A Note on Electricity

The electric charge of an atom is a result of the presence of negatively charged electrons and positively charged protons. The protons are generally tightly bound within the nucleus, but the electrons, especially those in the outermost "orbits"of the larger atoms, are capable of moving among the nearby atoms. They are essentially "free" electrons. When the electrons move, the electric charge moves and electromagnetic fields arise.

When an object with a negative charge (a surplus of electrons) gets close enough to an object with a positive charge (a deficit of electrons), there will be a spark when electrons jump from the negatively charged object to the positively charged one (lightning and static electricity).

Next, "When a voltage source is connected to a conductor, it applies a potential difference V that creates an electrical field. The electrical field, in turn, exerts force on free charges [electrons], causing current." Physics LibreTexts, "9.4: Resistivity and Resistance ," phys.libretexts.org, September 12, 2022.

When an energy differential is applied to one end of a conducting wire, free electrons at that end will be dislodged. They will then collide with electrons in the outer orbit of neighboring atoms, dislodging some others, which go on to collide with yet other electrons. The result is a ripple or "domino effect" causing some electrons at the other end of the wire to be ejected: An electric current. The dislodged electrons do not flow straight down the wire; they bounce around. However, the general movement of electrons will be down the wire. The current will appear to flow at close to the speed of light. A particular electron, however, is quite unlikely to travel straight down the wire. Instead, the electrons keep nudging their neighbors in that direction. The speed at which a particular electron moves down the wire is known as the "drift velocity."

"The high speed of electrical signals results from the fact that the electrons behave as an incompressible fluid. Thus, when a free charge is forced into a wire ... another leaves almost immediately, carrying the signal rapidly forward. The signal is passed on rapidly as an electrical shock wave moving through the system at nearly the speed of light."

University Physics, Volume 2, "9.2 Model of Conduction in Metals," *OpenStax*.

The number of electrons passing a particular point on the wire at a specific instance determines the number of amperes or "amps" of the current; the potential energy differential at the beginning of the wire (the stored energy/the capacity to do work) gives the voltage.

"A more concrete example of voltage from real life is a water tank with a hose extending from the bottom. Water in the tank represents stored charge. It takes work to fill the tank with water. ...The more water in the tank, the more pressure there is and the water can exit through the hose with more energy. ....This pressure potential is equivalent to voltage. The more water in the tank, the more pressure. The more charge stored in a battery, the more voltage."

Andrew Zimmerman Jones, "Voltage Definition in Physics," *ThoughtCo*, updated January 28, 2019.

CHAPTER 8

Maxima and Minima

"Profound equations are often said to be beautiful.
...If you look into the principle of least action
you are likely to be left rather solemnly silent."

Cormac McCarthy,
Stella Maris
(2022)

The seventeenth century science of "optics"—like astronomy—was one of the few sciences based on empirical observation and on empirical experimentation (although, more difficult in astronomy).

Snell's Law had provided a trigonometry-based formula for predicting the refraction of light traveling through different media. Pierre de Fermat provided an explanatory theory named Fermat's Principle of Least Time, which states that light traveling through different media will follow the path that takes the least amount of time. This principle predicted or reflected that light travels at different speeds through different media, like air and water. Thus, light traveling between a point in the air to a point in the water will follow a path such that the distance traveled through the air times the speed through the air plus the distance traveled through water times the speed through water is at the minimum (the least time) of all possible paths. *See* Richard Feyman, "Optics: The Principle of Least Time," *Feynman Lectures*, Vol. 1, No. 26 (1963, 2013).

Remarkable really.

In a segment of the story *Arrival*, introduced above, our scientists muse about scientific methodology.

Over Chinese food, Gary explains to Louise:

> "[W]hile the common formulation of physical laws is causal, a variational principle like Fermat's is purposive, al-most **teleological. ... [A]lmost every physical law could be stated as a variational principle.** Yet when humans thought about physical laws, they preferred to work with them in their causal formulation... ."

Id., p.121 (emphasis added).

As Richard Feynman observed in his famous lectures: "the principle of least time is a completely different philosophical principle about the way nature works. Instead of saying it is a causal thing, that when we do one thing, something else happens, and so on, it says this: we set up the situation, and light decides which is the shortest time, or the extreme one, and chooses that path."

Louise grasps the point: "[T]he ray of light has to know where it will ultimately end up before it can choose the direction to begin moving in... ." *Id.*, p.122.

She later muses:

> "[T]he physical attributes that humans found intuitive, like kinetic energy or acceleration, were all properties of an object at a given moment in time. And these were conducive to a chronological, causal interpretation of events: one moment growing out of another, causes and effects creating a chain reaction that grew from past to future."
>
> "...[B]ut, other attributes] were meaningful only over a period of time. And these were conducive to a teleological interpretation of events: by viewing events over a period of time, one recognized that there was a requirement that had to be satisfied, a goal of minimizing or maximizing. ...And one had to know the initial and final states to meet that goal; one needed knowledge of the effects before the causes could be initiated."

Chiang, *Arrival*, p.126.

As to Fermat, what is the contemporary scientific explanation of what happens? Feynman posed the question as follows: "But what does it do, how does it find out? Does it smell the nearby paths, and check them against each other? The answer is, yes, it does, in a way." One answer goes something like this: The light travels as a wave. When the first part of the wave reaches the detector, the wave "collapses" and the path established by, or determined in, that collapse is the one that got there first, the one that took the "least time."

Not really "sniffing out" the right path, but still pretty strange.

A similar example is photosynthesis.

"In that realm, electrons that have been excited by light are impossibly efficient at finding the fastest way to move from one part of a plant cell to another, seemingly because each electron does this by [presumably/possibly] being in a quantum superposition state, checking out all the possible routes at once."

Robert M. Sapolsky, *Determined: A Science of Life without Free Will* (2023), p.217.

Imagine if Gary is right that most Natural Laws have variational versions where, rather than "cause and effect," there is a seeking out of *minima* and/or *maxima*? We already have in "the calculus" the mathematical tools we would need, already used in classical physics. We just need new Laws or principles as alternatives to the old.

Well, it seems that there are such alternative theories.

"We have the common-sense notion of 'a straight line,' but two distinct ways of constructing it. One is 'keep moving in the same direction,' and the other is 'minimize the distance between your beginning and ending points.' The first way reflects a local philosophy of action, ...at every moment of time you're doing a particular thing, and by the end all of your effort has constructed a certain path. The second way is more global, ...of all possible ways a string could stretch between the two trees, you're choosing the one that is the shortest."

Sean M. Carroll, *The Biggest Ideas in the Universe: Space, Time, and Motion* (2023), p.55.

"At every point where the function is at a local maximum (the top of a hill) or minimum (the bottom of a valley), that derivative is exactly zero. ...That's the mathematical secret behind finding curves of minimum length, or any other property. ...So we can turn the verbal idea 'shortest-distance path' into a set of mathematical equations... ."

...

"What the particle will actually do is take the trajectory that minimizes its action... . ...What does it mean to minimize the action? The action is the integral of the Lagrangian, which is the kinetic energy minus potential energy. ...[M]ake the kinetic energy as small as we can."

...

"The least-action way of doing things is mathematically equivalent to Newton's original formulation. ...In the least-action approach, the word 'force' doesn't even appear anywhere."

...

"Our third way of formulating classical mechanics is Hamiltonian mechanics. Its central idea is to elevate "momentum" to a concept with an existence of its own, independent of 'velocity.' ...A particle (or more complicated system) has a location in space, and it also comes with a vector property, 'the momentum.' ...The Hamiltonian is basically the energy of the system, written in terms of the positions and momenta. ...In the space of all conceivable behaviors, there is no necessary relationship between position and momentum. But there are certain special trajectories, those that obey the equations of motion. And on those trajectories, momentum equals mass times velocity."

Carroll, *The Biggest Ideas*, pp.84, 85, 86, 87, 100, 102-3.

"This follows the principle that only that which exists maximally truly exists. None of the other ones exists intrinsically. This diktat is an example of a so-called extremum principle quite common in physics (e.g., the least action principle). ...Just as a bicycle chain held up at its two ends will naturally fold into the configuration that minimizes its potential energy without exhaustively trying out all possible configurations, so will the form that maximizes integrated information of a particular physical substrate. This form or structure exists, intrinsically, for itself."

Christof Koch, *Then I Am Myself the World: What Consciousness Is and How to Expand It* (2024), pp. 99, 101-102.

So,

"Does nature really start with some initial state and chug forward from moment to moment, as Laplace would have us believe? Or does nature have some kind of precognition, where it can visualize all the possible motions it might undertake between some initial point and some final point, and choose to move along the one that minimizes the action?

"Neither one. Nature just is nature, and it does what it does."

Carroll, *The Biggest Ideas*, p.88.

Well, perhaps.

So, there are such alternative theories, but they do not really imply teleology. What we really have are alternative ways of predicting what will happen. But, none tells us how the things that we can predict actually happen, or why. So, we should not get too concerned about the implications of alternative theories.

Let me say a little more about predictions and the question of how (and why). In a new book, *Determined: A Science of Life without Free Will* (2023), Robert M. Sapolsky discusses examples of emergent convergence. One is how colonies of ants apparently miraculously determine something close to the optimal route for connecting food sources or finding the best sites for new nests.

"[T]ake the roughly ten thousand ants in a typical colony, set them loose on the eight-feeding-site version, and they'll come up with something close to the optimal solution out of the 5,040 possibilities in a fraction of the time it would take you to brute-force it, with no ant knowing anything ... ."

...

"[E]ach ant then picks a route at random that involves visiting each site once, and leaves a pheromone trail in the process... .. ...The shorter the route, the thicker the pheromone trail that is laid down by a scout; pheromones evaporate, and thus shorter, thicker pheromone trails last longer. A second generation of ants shows up; they wander randomly, with the rule that if they encounter a pheromone trail, they join it, adding their own pheromones. As a result, the thicker and therefore longer-lasting the trail, the more likely another ant is to join it and amplify its recruiting message. And soon the less efficient routes for connecting the sites evaporate away... ."

Id., pp.158, 162.

They do not explore and compare all options, as humans may do. Instead, Sapolsky says, they "utilize" a system of scouts and broadcasts causing the mass of ants to be "drawn" to the best route or location, all without any intent or decision-making. I leave the description of the supposed mechanics of this accomplishment to Sapolsky and his sources, but there are important, actually crucial common features among this example and the many others.

The key is the existence of a system that automatically (without intent) produces incentives (or coercion) pulling or pushing the individual elements in the right directions. That requires some method(s) of measurement or assessment and some means of communication.

"[A] number of motifs ... come into play in emergent systems—rich-get-richer phenomena where higher-quality solutions give off stronger recruiting signals, iterative bifurcation that inserts near-infinity into finite places, spatiotemporal control of attraction and repulsion rules, mathematical optimizing of the balance between different wiring needs... ." *Id.*, p.187.

The question then becomes how such systems come to exist. In the biological world, the accepted answer is "through evolution." Random changes allow the "testing" of incomprehensible number of alternatives. The winner in the struggle for survival will be the organism that emerges, not with the best solution to its immediate challenge, but with the system or structure that allows the identification of the best solutions to similar challenges as they arise. (I discuss at length the essential features and limitations of Darwinian evolution in *Important Things*.)

Curiously, optimization processes also exist in the nonliving world too. How can they come into being? I discuss that matter in *Important Things*, as well. Now, none of this is actually relevant to this essay except as a means of clarifying the distinction I make between theories that are able to predict accurately and those that can seem to explain.

CHAPTER 9

A Note on Life

"A life within a life.
An independent living being
—a unit—that forms a part of the whole.
A living building block
contained within the larger living being."

Siddhartha Mukherjee
*The Song of the Cell:
An Exploration of Medicine
and the New Human*
(2022), p.xiv.

"'Each cell leads a double life,'
[Matthias] Schleiden would write ... [in 1838],
'an entirely independent one,
belonging to its own development alone;
and an incidental one,
in so far as it has become part of a plant.'"

Id., p.xiii.

I have discussed previously Schrödinger's famous essay "What is Life?" *Important Things*, pp.236-7, 283, 286, 289, 536. I return to the central issue raised in that essay—how is life even possible?

He began:

> "The large and important and very much discussed question is: How can the events in space and time which take place within the spatial boundary of a living organism be accounted for by physics and chemistry?
>
> ...
>
> "The arrangements of the atoms in the most vital parts of an organism and the interplay of these arrangements differ in a fundamental way from all those arrangements of atoms which physicists and chemists have hitherto made the object of their experimental and theoretical research."
>
> ...
>
> "It is by avoiding the rapid decay into the inert state of 'equilibrium' that an organism appears so enigmatic... ."

Schrödinger, "What is Life? The Physical Aspect of the Living Cell" (1944).

"[W]hat puzzled Schrödinger about life was ... [h]ow can organisms exhibit predictable and orderly structures and behaviours if they are based on physical and chemical laws that are statistical, such that one might expect any orderliness to be 'perpetually disturbed and made inoperative by the unceasing heat motion of the atoms'?"

Philip Ball, "Life does not run like clockwork," *CHEMISTRYWORLD*, 16 March 2022.

The issue is how does sufficient stability for life arise from phenomena that are inherently random. Schrödinger's answer is the so-called Law of Large Numbers, an averaging effect that permits the underlying tendencies to emerge and dominate. This concept suggests why it is that living organisms are so phenomenally large compared to atoms—it requires tens of millions of atoms for the random behavior of individual atoms to be statistically neutralized.

"Only in the co-operation of an enormously large number of atoms do statistical laws begin to operate and control the behaviour of these assemblies with an accuracy increasing as the number of atoms involved increases. It is in that way that the events acquire truly orderly features. All the physical and chemical laws that are known to play an important part in the life of organisms are of this statistical kind... ."

...

"[A]n organism must have a comparatively gross structure in order to enjoy the benefit of fairly accurate laws, both for its internal life and for its interplay with the external world. For otherwise the number of co-operating particles would be too small, the 'law' too inaccurate... ."

Schrödinger, "What is Life?"

Philip Ball suggests that an answer could be found in "causal emergence:"

"Causal emergence doesn't just mean that we can conveniently carve up the complex system into meaningful large-scale aggregates of the microscopic particles... . It also gives these systems a valuable new property: **insensitivity to microscale noise.**"

Id.

Or, in Giorgio Parisi's description of his efforts:

"We wanted to find a formalism that, **starting from this known microscopic description, would be able to describe the system at an intermediate level without referring to microscopic details... .** At this intermediate, or mesoscopic, level, we study the fluctuations of the system: groups of more or less numerous atoms passing from one phase to another. ...Every time we do this, we are actually changing the scale and significantly reducing the number of variables to be taken into consideration."

In a Flight of Starlings: The Wonders of Complex Systems (2023), pp.56, 59 (emphasis added).

All three of these explanations address the elimination of micro-level noise. The next question is what enables stability. Schrödinger finds the key in the quantum nature of reality. If energy levels were continuous, we would all be sliding down the slippery slopes leading to complete disorder and equilibrium. Instead, atoms and molecules change energy levels in discreet steps, like stairs, so there will be the stability to withstand constant small perpetrations without changing, and ther will be valleys where equilibrium obtains.

> "[T]o reconcile the high durability of the hereditary substance with its minute size, we had to evade the tendency to disorder by 'inventing the molecule', in fact, an unusually large molecule which has to be a masterpiece of highly differentiated order, **safeguarded by the conjuring rod of quantum theory**."
>
> Schrödinger, "What is Life?" (emphasis added).

The most interesting question is what causes or directs the macro-level behavior. What is the source of those macro-level tendencies? Traditional physics does not purport to answer the "why" or, often, even the "how," only the "what".

The miracle of the genome.

> "[I]ncredibly small groups of atoms, much too small to display exact statistical laws, do play a dominating role in the very orderly and lawful events within a living organism. They have control of the observable large-scale features which the organism acquires in the course of its development, they determine important characteristics of its functioning... .
>
> ...
>
> "A single group of atoms existing only in one copy produces orderly events, marvellously tuned in with each other and us number of with the environment according to most subtle laws.
>
> ...
>
> However, it needs no poetical imagination but only clear and sober scientific reflection to recognize that we are here obviously faced with events whose regular and lawful unfolding is guided by a 'mechanism' entirely different from the 'probability mechanism' of physics ... that a small but highly organized group of atoms be capable of acting in this manner, the situation is unprecedented, it is unknown anywhere else except in living matter."

Schrödinger, "What is Life?"

With biological structures, where the behavior can be attributed to a mechanistic arrangement that can be achieved through a series of random changes, the accepted answer is evolution—the survival of arrangements that promote survival and reproduction of the organism.

"We have built a machine on both the level of neurons communicating with each other in a circuit and the level of chemical changes inside a single key neuron. This is a machine that is entirely mechanistic in biological terms and that changes adaptively in response to a changing environment... .

...

"Think about this. Humans, being conditioned to blink their eyes, and marine sea slugs, conditioned to withdraw their gills, haven't shared a common ancestor for more than half a billion years. And here we are, with their neurons and ours using the same intracellular machinery for changing in response to experience."

Robert M. Sapolsky, *Determined: A Science of Life without Free Will* (2023), pp.278. 283.

Okay, up to a point.

The problem and the challenge is that we have been unable to identify mechanistic models for life or for various key characteristics like consciousness, creativity, intelligence, free will and, even, rationality.

CHAPTER 10

Beauty and Truth

"Beauty in mathematics.
Yes. Is that a part of its description?
Is that what makes it true?
Profound equations are
often said to be beautiful."

...

"Are the equations themselves beautiful?
Not if you dont know what they mean."

Cormac McCarthy
Stella Maris, pp.68, 69.

Since the beginning of the Scientific Revolution, many scientists have believed that one characteristic of a good or true scientific theory was elegance or beauty. Admittedly, a bit elusive to define, but something we would know when we see it. Initially, that belief presumably had theological roots, expectations about God's design of the World, but it has lived on with no explanatory basis, other than faith based on experience. Rationally, this belief should be found mainly among those who demand understanding from science, not satisfied with mere accuracy of predictions; but I have detected no such correlation.

Of course, a subjective or human-based criterion like beauty seems odd in the context of science. There have been attempts to define beauty and even to make it quantifiable. Obviously, it must be more than simplicity, which, like Occam's Razor, is inherently relative. Twentieth-century scientists have talked of "rigidity," meaning that the whole theory collapses if one removes a piece of it. That does not suggest "beauty" to me, however. Another term used is "naturalness," referring to the absence of contrived or "fine-tuned" elements or parameters. That is better, but incomplete.

A scientist turned writer, Sabine Hossenfelder, wrote a book a few years ago purporting to show that physicists' preoccupation or obsession with beauty was hampering scientific advancement. She explains:

> "Mathematical rigidity I had to discard because it rests on the selection of *a priori* truths, a choice that is itself not rigid, turning the idea into an absurdity. Neither could I find a mathematical basis for simplicity, naturalness, or elegance, each of which in the end brought back subjective, human values. In using these criteria, I fear, we overstep the limits of science."

Sabine Hossenfelder, *Lost in Math: How Beauty Leads Physics Astray* (2018), p.94.

Her principal example is from her own experience. She asserts that the continuing pursuit of certain proposed theoretical additions to particle physics, despite some 30 years of empirical failures, because they would be beautiful and elegant if true.

However, she is unable to propose any ugly theory that has been ignored yet could do the job. She similarly fails to provide evidence that those toiling away so far in vain could have been more productively employed. Finally, she does not argue, or substantiate the argument, that a useful theory is likely to be rejected if it is ugly.*

But, she does ponder this intriguing philosophical question: "I already know that the world embodies beautiful ideas. I want to know whether the world embodies ugly ideas, and if so, **whether we would continue to think of them as ugly**." *Id.*, p.145 (emphasis added).

Perhaps, beauty is truth, but is truth necessarily beautiful? For example, do we see truth as beauty? Or, the gaining of insight as beautiful?

"When trying to get a concrete understanding of real processes, everything seems incredibly complicated—but as soon as the work is completed, it seems beautifully simple. When we study a physics theory or a mathematical theorem in a textbook, everything seems perfectly clear. The amount of complicated work that was necessary to obtain the result has completely disappeared."

Giorgio Parisi, *In a Flight of Starlings: The Wonders of Complex Systems* (2023), p.78.

Her other examples tend to fall into the realm of cosmology, where it is normal for a handful of empirical observations to support a vast theoretical structure. "Again we see that it's a reliance on mathematics together with a desire for simplicity that leads to multiple universes." *Id.*, p.104. So, string theory, inflation, dark matter, dark energy and multiple universes. The proponents of those theories say: "'It's not us; it's **the math that made us do it. And math doesn't lie.** We are merely being objective, good scientists, they say. If you're opposing these insights, you are in denial and just refuse to accept inconvenient logical consequences.'" *Id.*102 (emphasis added).

"String theory is beginning to look like endless mathematics. That's the principal complaint I suppose. One of the first things that showed up in the equations was a particle of zero mass, zero charge, and spin two. Pretty promising. A graviton. Yes. A creature imagined but never seen."

...

"The reason for point particles is that if you stick something ugly in there—such as physical reality—the equations dont work. A point devoid of physical being leaves you with location. ...[T]he whole idea of point particles is contrary to common sense. Something is there."

Cormac McCarthy, *The Passenger* (2022), pp.146, 149.

Yet, the problem with the multiple universes and similar is not that the theorists favored beauty over truth. It is that they ignore the scientific standard of empirical falsifiability. Indeed, they even dispense with empirical confirmability. It seems to suffice to be able to say "nothing proves me wrong."

"[A] bit like Dirac. Or Chandrasekhar. He had an abiding faith in the aesthetic. He thought the Higgs paper too elegant to be wrong. For instance. You can add Glashow's SU(5) theory to the list. Lovely theory. And wrong." McCarthy, *The Passenger,* p.152.

In the modern view, beauty is relative, culturally determined. In fact, we are suppose to believe that all value systems are relative and, perhaps, equal. So, what about truth? So, is truth culturally determined? Is one person's truth as good as any other's? Well, our concept of truth is certainly homocentric. It is culturally influenced. Yet, we resist. The danger is the loss of what Frank Wilczek referred to as "the style of thought that allowed us to discover" the facts of nature—the scientific method. Of course, again, scientific progress has arisen, and can continue to arise, from the investigation of speculative hypotheses. And, it often takes much time and many false starts. Also, the devising of empirical test can require time, ingenuity and skill.

"...[B]are facts about how the physical world works ... are both powerful and strangely beautiful, to be sure. But the style of thought that allowed us to discover them is a great achievement, too."

Frank Wilczek, *Fundamentals: Ten Keys to Reality* (2022), p.xi.

So, beauty.

Astrophysicist/Blogger Ethan Siegel asserts:

"...[I]f you have multiple different models that have different underlying assumptions that go into them, there's a scientific way to tell which one is superior. It isn't to look at personal preference, elegance, aesthetics, or simplicity. Instead, there are two key questions that we have to evaluate.
Which theory has fewer free parameters?
Which theory better fits the full suite of data concerning the Universe?
... [A] theory that can make the same predictions as another but with fewer assumptions or required inputs is a superior physical theory to one that requires more assumptions, required inputs, or free parameters."

Ethan Siegel, "Is the Universe 13.8 or 26.7 billion years old?" *Big Think: Starts with a Bang,* July 18, 2023.

Is his "fewer parameters" criteria really so different?

"In physics, of course, the proof is in the testing, not in the beauty, regardless of what some people might whimsically wish." Lawrence M. Krauss, *The Edge of Knowledge: Unsolved Mysteries of the Cosmos* (2023), p.103.

"...[B]eauty can be a treacherous guide in science, as in life." Nick Lane, *Transformer: The Deep Chemistry of Life and Death* (2023), p. 128.

REALITY

And, then there is the question of the reality of truth. Is there such a thing as truth? If so, can we ever find it? Or, will it always be receding just out of our reach? Is truth like an elusive idea? Like a dream that is always vanishing?

"'Evanescent as a rainbow... . It is a thing that was known, but, from the moment consciousness turned its lantern upon it, began to become invisible. ... [I]t seems only to be turning corner after corner to evade the mind's eye, but behind every corner it leaves a portion of itself; until at length ... it is gone so utterly that the mind remains aghast in the perplexity of the doubt whether ever there was a thought there at all."

George McDonald, *Thomas Wingfold, Curate* (1876) (Kindle 2012), loc.4561.

"And I woke up and as I woke up the dream began to dissolve. The dream and the story of the dream. And I knew that in the dream was an

---

understanding that was simply a gift and it was receding in the darkness and I sat up in bed and called out after it but it simply fell to pieces in my mind... ."

McCarthy, *Stella Maris*, p.181.

The question of "what is reality" is difficult. It is hard to know whether one should look to philosophers, neuroscientists, physicists, cosmologists or novelists for the answer.

Some examples.

The novelist:

"You will never know what the world is made of. The only thing that's certain is that it's not made of the world. As you close upon some mathematical description of reality you cant help but lose what is being described. Every inquiry displaces what is addressed. A moment in time is a fact, not a possibility. The world will take your life. But above all and lastly the world does not know that you are here. You think that you understand this. But you dont."

McCarthy, *The Passenger,* p.128.

The cosmologists?

They bring us a new possibility—that the Universe is really just a 3D hologram.

"[I]n 1997 ... Juan Maldacena ... create[d] a mathematical model of **the entire universe as a hologram**. ...**[A]ll the information about what happens inside some volume of space is encoded as quantum fields on the surface of the region's boundary.** ...Galaxies, black holes, gravity, stars and the rest, including us, are ... inside, and **the information describing them resides on the outside... .**"

Dennis Overbye, "Black Holes May Hide a Mind-Bending Secret About Our Universe," *NYT.com*, October 12, 2022 (emphasis added).

And,

"Today, the holographic revolution in physics is turning Plato's vision on its head. The latest incarnation of holography envisions that everything in the four dimensions we experience is in fact a manifestation of a hidden reality located on a thin slice of spacetime."

Thomas Hertog, *On the Origin of Time* (2023), p.212. (Discussed further in another essay.)

Now, how about that?

Beautiful?

Hmmm... .

In his famous lectures on physics at Cal'Tech, Richard Feynman presented a seventeenth century illustration:

> "When a new theoretical principle is developed, such as the [Fermat's] principle of least time, our first inclination might be to say, 'Well, that is **very pretty**; it is delightful; but the question is, does it help at all in understanding the physics?' Someone may say, 'Yes, look at how many things we can now understand!' Another says, 'Very well, but I can understand mirrors... [and] lens, too, because every ray that comes to it is bent through an angle given by Snell's law.'"

Feynman then asked and answered:

> **"So is it merely a philosophical question,**
> **or one of beauty?**
> **There can be arguments on both sides."**

"Optics," *Feynman Lectures*, Vol. 1, No. 26 (1963) (emphasis added).

---

* I have been critical of Sabine Hossenfelder's book, but my dissatisfaction is entirely with the theme identified in the title, which I assume was selected in the belief that it would sell books (if you do not have sex or an attack on religion, a criticism of mathematical science may be the next best thing). The preponderance of the book itself, however, is an excellent discussion of the Standard Model of Particle Physics and potential revisions to it. Possibly, the best I have read.

Determinism

CHAPTER 11

Probability

PROBABILITY

Probability is a uniquely human construct, both in conception and in practice. Even in theory, it exists only in the context of repeatable, controlled experiments, the best examples of which are games of chance, whether based on cards or dice or the flip of a coin or spin of a wheel. The probabilities reflect the likelihood that certain outcomes will occur if a particular action is taken. They are predictive only, reflecting what is expected to happen over many trials.The concept can also be used in connection with the number of items with a certain characteristic (say, red in color) included in a larger collection of similar (but, not red) items to represent the likelihood that a random selection from the larger collection will result in (or yield) a red one. *See* Steven Pinker, *Rationality: What It Is, Why It Seems Scarce, Why It Matters* (2021), pp. 113-8.

Now, the important point is that the probability is not a characteristic of a thing or object itself ("probabilities are not about the world; they're about our ignorance of the world. ...New information reduces our ignorance and changes the probability" *id.*, p.22). Similarly, it is rather odd (although, quite common) to talk about the probability of a one time event ("the vaguely mystical notion of the probability of a single instance" *id.*, p.115). The event either happens or it does not. And, it is also strange to ask "what is the probability that Jack is taller than Jill?"; although, in certain contexts, it could be a legitimate question (for example, if all you know about them is their sex or, for a more difficult question, their sex and Jill's height).

Again, such a probability is not a part of Jack nor of Jill.

The theory of the calculation of probabilities (developed in the seventeenth century by the Reverend Thomas Bayes) is not intuitive, is not part of our innate mental toolkit, so it can provide some surprising information. An example, set out by Steven Pinker, with slightly different numbers, asks "What is the probability that X has cancer given that he tested positive?" where 2 out of 100 people have cancer (2%), the sensitivity of the test is 95% (where the patient has cancer, the test will be positive 95% of the time and fail to detect it 5% of the time) and the incidence of false positives from the test is 1 out 10 or 10%. *Id.*, pp150-3. Is it 90%?

No, not even close. The probability that X has cancer given that he tested positive, according to the Rev. Bayes, is the sum of the probability that someone in the group has cancer (2%) multiplied by the probability that someone who tests positive has cancer (90%) divided by the sum of the probability of getting a positive result if someone has cancer (95% of the 2% who have cancer or 1.9%) plus the probability of a positive result if someone does not have cancer (10%). That gives us .02 x 0.9 = .018, divided by .019 + .1 (or .119), for a probability of 15.2%.

Surprised?

Think of it this way. If you tested all 100 men, you would likely get almost 10 false positives (98 times 10%) and almost 2 actual or correct positives (the 2 men with cancer times the test sensitivity of 95%). In other words, the likelihood of false positives greatly exceeds the likelihood of any one man having cancer. ("In the world of Bayes, 'likelihood' is not a synonym for 'probability,' but refers to how likely it is that the data would turn up if the hypothesis is true." *Id.*, p.152.)

This result crucially depends on the selection of our test case from out of the 100 candidates being random. Suppose, instead, X was one of 15 men who got selected to be tested and that we knew that 25% of people selected to be tested would turn out to have cancer. Then, the probability that X has cancer, being one of the selected and testing positive, is 25% times 90% (or 22.5%) divided by 95% times 25% plus 10% times 75% (that is, 31.25%), or 72%.

What can we infer from the fact that the calculations above are not intuitive? Perhaps, that the calculation of conditional probabilities had little relevance for survival or reproduction in the early years of human development. But, it does have relevance to our decision-making in today's world.

I noted that probability does not appear to be part of our natural world. Yet, "In the second half of the nineteenth century, James Clerk Maxwell and Ludwig Boltzmann, apparently independently, created statistical mechanics introducing probability and statistics into physics at the microscopic level, with the express purpose of understanding collective behavior." Giorgio Parisi, *In a Flight of Starlings: The Wonders of Complex Systems* (2023), p.85.

Moreover, "[t]he actual world is disordered, and as we said at the start, many situations in the real world can be described as a large number of elementary agents that interact with each other. These interactions can be schematized with simple rules, but the results of their collective action are sometimes really unpredictable." *Id.*, p.80.

Curiously, probability also arises prominently in our best current scientific theory of elemental particles—quantum mechanics. For example, "[q]uantum mechanics tells us the probability that, upon observing a quantum system with a specified wave function, we will see any particular outcome." Sean M. Carroll, *The Big Picture: On the Origins of Life, Meaning, and the Universe Itself* (2016), p.163.

"In quantum mechanics, the state of a system is a superposition of all the possible measurement outcomes, known as the 'wave function' of the system. The wave function is a combination of every result you could get by doing an observation, with **different weights for each possibility.**"

...

"[E]ven in interpretations where wave functions really do collapse when systems are observed, the person doing the observing has no influence whatsoever on what the measurement outcome turns out to be. That just follows a rule, the Born rule for quantum probabilities, which says **the probability of each outcome is given by the value of the wave function squared**. ... Just physics."

Id., pp.162, 367 (emphasis added).

As I previously wrote, quoting another contemporary physicist:

"Max Born proposed in 1926 that the wave pattern (the 'mist' or 'cloud') that was part of the emitted particle represented probabilities of where the particle would be found, so that the more intense or thicker part of the 'mist' was where the probability of finding the particle was greater and in the more dispersed portions of the 'mist,' the probabilities were less. Julian Barbour, *The End of Time*, p.198. ...'[T]he probabilities reflect a fundamental property of nature, not simply our ignorance.' *Id.*, p.203. It is not the case that before the measurement of the particle (*e.g.*, before it hits the screen), it has a particular position and 'momentum but we just do not know it'; it is that preceding measurement 'all momenta...are present as potentialities, and measurement forces one of them to be actualized.' *Id.*, p.203."

Important Things, p.360.

An alternative possibility was noted by astrophysicist Adam Frank—that probabilities reflect not the physical world, but only our knowledge of it. In reviewing a 2019 book by Sean Carroll, Frank wrote: that he favors "Quantum Baysianism... . This theory states that the equations of quantum mechanics are always about our knowledge of the electron not the electron by itself... ." "In 'Something Deeply Hidden,' Sean Carroll Argues There Are Infinite Copies Of You,' *NPR*, September 13, 2019.

Does this view undermine or promote quantum mechanics?

So, is probability, in fact, a fundamental part of quantum reality?

"It wasnt just the quantum dice that disturbed Einstein. It was the whole underlying notion. The indeterminacy of reality itself." McCarthy, *The Passenger*, p.147.

"For Einstein, quantum mechanics was not the whole story. He contested in particular the Copenhagen school's interpretation, in which probability plays a fundamental role: physical theory just had to be deterministic." Parisi, *In a Flight of Starlings*, p.90.

"One of the many misstatements about quantum mechanics is that it is not deterministic. This is incorrect. Quantum mechanics is based on an equation that describes the time evolution of the wavefunction. This means that if one specifies the value of a wavefunction at some initial time, its value at all subsequent times can be determined exactly, at least in principle. The wavefunction, defined more precisely, gives the probability amplitude (a complex number) of finding the system in a certain state. The square of the wavefunction gives the probability (a real number between zero and one) of measuring the system to be each of its many possible allowed states. Quantum mechanics determines these probabilities exactly."

Lawrence M. Krauss, *The Edge of Knowledge: Unsolved Mysteries of the Cosmos* (2023) (Kindle), loc.1865-7.

Still, probabilities.

CHAPTER 12

"Poetic Naturalism"

"[T]there is only one world, the natural world,
exhibiting patterns we call the 'laws of nature,'
and which is discoverable by
the methods of science and empirical investigation."

Carroll, *The Big Picture*, p.11.

This book (Sean M. Carroll, *The Big Picture: On the Origins of Life, Meaning, and the Universe Itself*) was published in 2016, contemporaneously with the first edition of my *Important Things We Don't Know* (then, entitled *Limits of Science?*). It so happened that we addressed several of the same topics and did so in similar ways. However, Carroll went quite a different direction than I did, with a different objective. His goal was to argue that his version of determinism, which he calls "poetic naturalism," is consistent with the existence of life, of consciousness and even, perhaps, of free will, but not with a soul nor immortality nor even, perhaps, God. I, in contrast, was highly critical of determinism.

Carroll asserts:

> "[T]he entirety of both the past and future history are utterly determined by the present. ...By the 'state' of the universe, or any subsystem thereof, we mean the position and the velocity of every particle within it."
>
> ...
>
> "Together, you give me the state of the universe at one time, and I can use the laws of physics to integrate forward (or backward) and get the state of the universe at any other time."

Id., pp.32, 33.

That is surely determinism. ("It's perfectly deterministic, even though individual observers can't tell which world they are in before they actually look at it, so there is necessarily some probabilistic component when it comes to people making predictions." *Id.*, p.169.)

Yet, there is more to say. "Quantum mechanics, at least the way we teach it to physics majors taking their first college courses in the subject, says that there are two completely different ways that the state of a system evolves over time." *Id.*, p.164.

He explains:

> "One kind of evolution happens when we're not observing the system. ...Evolution according to the Schrödinger equation is very much like the evolution of a state in classical mechanics. It is smooth, reversible, and **completely deterministic...** ."

...

"[A]n entirely different way the quantum state can evolve, according to the textbook treatment: namely, when it is observed ... the wave function 'collapses,' and we obtain some particular measurement outcome. The ... evolution is **nondeterministic**—knowing what the state was before, you can't perfectly predict what the state will be afterward. **All you have are probabilities.**"

Id., pp.164, 165 (emphasis added).

Thus, "[o]ne approach is to suggest that while the wave function plays an important role in predicting experimental outcomes, it doesn't actually represent physical reality," which was the view of Niels Bohr. *Id.*, p166. But, Carroll says, "[t]he simplest possibility is that the quantum wave function isn't a bookkeeping device at all, nor is it one of many kinds of quantum variables; **the wave function simply represents reality directly.**" *Id.*, p.167 (emphasis added).

He supports his view with the work of Hugh Everett III. "Everett suggests, the wave function doesn't collapse into one possibility or the other. It evolves smoothly into an entangled superposition... . Both parts of the superposition actually exist, and they continue to exist and evolve as the Schrödinger equation demands." *Id.*, p.169. This theory leads to the "multiverse," a theory that I have previously critiqued.

Carroll also asserts that all there is are fields. Pierre-Simon Laplace proposed over two hundred years ago that "Newtonian gravity could be thought of as a field theory, positing a 'gravitational potential field' that filled all of space, thereby resolving Newton's puzzlement about actions at a distance between faraway bodies." *Id.*, p.31.

Today, physicists conclude that every thing consists of fields, even particles:

> "Our best theory of the world—at least in the domain of applicability that includes our everyday experience—takes unification one step further, to say that both particles and forces arise out of fields. ...Modern physics says that the particles and the forces that make up atoms all arise out of fields. That viewpoint is called quantum field theory."

Id., p.172.

In my book, I had asked what are fields? Carroll has this answer: "[A] field has a value at every single point in space—that's just what a field is. *Id.* "And what are the fields made of? There isn't any such thing. The fields are the stuff that everything else is made of." *Id.* "Another feature of quantum field theory is that you can't turn the forces from individual particles on and off; the associated fields are always there." *Id.*, p.184. Just about what I said, but I expressed skepticism about the supposed "reality" of fields.

Finally, Carroll is quite skeptical of "strong emergence" (where emergent properties are not somehow contained in the pre-emergent circumstances). He seems to believe that emergent properties are always there but just not observable. *See id.*, pp.108-10.

Carroll explains, surely correctly, that theories can exist on different levels. A higher-level theory may be extremely successful at making predictions and "explaining" what we observe, yet be literally inconsistent with an equally successful lower-level theory. Examples include the "gene" and classical mechanics. The different levels have different vocabularies, using different words, because they describe different things. The higher levels recognize emergent phenomena.

Interestingly, Carroll argues that these emergent phenomena are "real," which is the "poetic" part of his poetic naturalism, but he continues to be unclear whether by "real" he means something that physically exists or just something that should be taken seriously.

> "[O]ur fundamental ontology, the best way we have of talking about the world at the deepest level, is extremely sparse. But many concepts that are part of non-fundamental ways we have of talking about the world—useful ideas describing higher-level, macroscopic reality—deserve to be called 'real'."

Id., p19.

But, he regularly says things like: "At the deepest level we currently know about, [there are] [n]o causes, whether material, formal, efficient, or final. But there are levels on top of that, where the vocabulary changes. ...[I]t's so useful to refer to causes and effects in our everyday experience, even if they're not present in the underlying equations." *Id.*, p.29. And, "human agency, our ability to make choices about what to do next. As we'll see, that's not really an issue of physics, but one of description: What is the best way we have to talk about human beings?" *Id.*, p.32. Or, "the notion of a ship is a derived category in our ontology, not a fundamental one. It is a useful way of talking about certain subsets of the basic stuff of the universe." *Id.*, p.17.

Time

Carroll concludes that at a fundamental level, there is no separate past or future, only the present, which incorporates the past and the future. The elemental particles and the four forces are timeless, that is, they exist without time. At the fundamental level, the Universe is, therefore, timeless. The Core Theory (The Standard Model plus General Relatively, so named by Frank Wilczek, *id.*, p.176) does not include time. There is no past and no future, only the now.

Yet, he observes that life is "a process." Of course, a process presumes the existence of time since it is something that occurs over time.

"We won't really live forever, no matter how clever biologists get to be. Everybody dies. **Life is not a substance, like water or rock; it's a process,** like fire or a wave crashing on the shore. It's a process that begins, lasts for a while, and ultimately ends. Long or short, our moments are brief against the expanse of eternity." *Id.*, p.2 (emphasis added).

Carroll acknowledges that something must be added to the Core Theory. That something is a very special "initial condition," the state of extraordinary low entropy. Given the assumption that the Universe started in such an unusual state, then time will necessarily "emerge" as an characteristic of the Universe that follows.

The "thing we need to add is an assumption about the initial condition of the observable universe, namely, that it was in a very low-entropy state. The origin of time's arrow, therefore, is ekinological: it arises from a special condition in the far past. Amazingly, it seems that this property of entropy is responsible for all of the differences between past and future that we know about." *Id.*, p.58.

Presumably, Carroll includes The Second Law of Thermodynamics as an applicable Law of Nature, even though it has no relevance to his fundamental reality. Carroll also provides no explanation for the highly unusual initial state of the Universe. It is just a given.

Carroll asserts:

"The current state, by itself, constrains the past and future equally. But the current state plus the hypothesis of a low-entropy past gives us enormous leverage over the actual history of the universe. It's that leverage that lets us believe (often correctly) that our memories are reliable guides to what actually happened. ...[T]he origin of that arrow is that we know something specific and informative about the past (it had a low entropy), but there is no corresponding statement we can make about the future."

Id., p.66 (emphasis added).

However, we do know that the future will have very high entropy. What is so different?

So, is the emergent "time" something real or is it just a convenient and useful tool?

Design

Like I did, Carroll uses Star Trek's famous transporter capability as an example (see "Beam me up, Scotty" in my chapter on Consciousness, *Important Things*, p.471). Carroll concludes that, as long as we do not get multiple Captain Kirks, it does not much matter whether the transporter reuses the original atoms to reconstruct Kirk or utilizes new ones. That makes sense. "If there were just a single copy, most of us would have no trouble accepting them as the original person. (Using different atoms doesn't really matter; in actual human bodies, our atoms are lost and replaced all the time.)" *Id.*, p.15.

But, he says nothing about the thing that matters most—the design that establishes the arrangement of those atoms. It was certainly an emergent phenomenon at some point. Is that something real? Is that something contained in the Core Theory plus the initial conditions?

Things

So, starting from a very low-entropy state, the entropy of the Universe begins to increase as something unknown propels the fields apart. Some of the fields appear as particles. Somehow, atoms form, and gravity starts to affect them and certain of the particles. What we call (for convenience) "matter" starts forming in clumps. From this point on, we have a pretty good idea what happens next to produce stars, galaxies and planets, as well as the elements, including heavy metals. Then what?

Carroll notes that we can find numerous examples of matter self-organizing itself into patterns or structures, like crystals or snowflakes. ("In the right circumstances, matter self-organizes into intricate configurations, capable of capturing and using information from their environments. The culmination of this process is life itself." *Id.*, p.5) That is correct, and in several cases, we can even explain why. But, we lack a general theory of why in certain instances as the entropy of the whole continuously increases until equilibrium is reached, in places, locally it increases. It is in those situations that "things" come into existence.

Carroll spends a lot of time hypothesizing how many small steps can lead to major changes, like in Darwin's theories; but, he lacks the driving forces of those theories: scarcity, competition, replication and variation. Thus, the most we can say is that it could happen, not whether it will nor why. Moreover, Carroll ignores a prominent feature of Darwinism, its inherent randomness, which is fundamentally inconsistent with determinism.

Consciousness

Finally, Carroll addresses consciousness. He does not try to define it, just suggests characteristics. He certainly does not attempt to explain how it came to be. But, he observes how useful it is to have and to use the concept of consciousness, which fact in his poetic naturalism makes it "real."

Does that mean it exists?

"[T'he emergent theory describes true features of the system that might be completely hidden from the microscopic point of view. From that perspective—the correct one—we really do learn something new by studying emergent theories for their own sakes, even if all the theories are utterly compatible."

.....

"In strong emergence, the behavior of a system with many parts is not reducible to the aggregate behavior of all those parts, even in principle. The only way to think of it is as an effect of the whole on the individual parts.If it's how the world actually does work, then our purported microscopic theory of the atom is simply wrong."

Id., pp.108, 109.

Carroll discusses a thought experiment set out by David Chalmers about zombies. It proposes beings that are just like humans physically and behaviorally but that are not conscious. If they "could" exist, then consciousness would seem not to be a physical characteristic.

"David Chalmers ... is arguably the leading modern advocate for the possibility that physical reality needs to be augmented by some kind of additional ingredient in order to explain consciousness... ." *Id.,* p.355.

Carroll suggests that if such zombies were to exist, then there would have to be physical differences between them and us. That seems to beg the question. More to the point, he says that such zombies could not exist because entities without consciousness would necessarily behave differently than beings that are conscious. "The problem is that the notion of 'inner mental states' isn't one that merely goes along for the ride as we interact with the world. It has an important role to play in accounting for how people behave." *Id.*, p.358.

Initially, that seems right and dispositive.

Then, he seems to lose the thread, saying:

> "The big question about zombies is a simple one: can they possibly exist? If they can, it's a knockout argument against the idea that consciousness can be explained in completely physical terms. **If you can have two identical collections of atoms,** both of which take the form of a human being, but **one has consciousness and the other does not, then consciousness cannot be purely physical.**"

Id., p.356 (emphasis added).

But, what about behavior?

The problem is that in the hypothetical, the zombies behave just like the conscious people. So, if asked "Are you a zombie?" the zombie will answer (falsely) "no" (or, "Do you have feelings?" "Yes.").

By what mechanism is that false answer generated?

"There are no internal, conscious experiences at all. It is a world of zombies (except they look just like us, even say the same things, and so on). ...[N]euron A causes neuron B to fire, and so on, in the same great web of extrinsic material patterns of this world, but in the zombie world there is no associated experience."

Erik Hoel, *The World Behind the World: Consciousness, Free Will, and the Limits of Science* (2023), p.125.

Actually, the important question is by what mechanism does your feelings or subjective state cause behavior. The question is how the non-material affects the material.

"If these mental properties affected the behavior of particles in the same way that physical properties like mass and electric charge do, then they would simply be another kind of physical property. You are free to postulate new properties that affect the behavior of electrons and photons, but you're not simply adding new ideas to the Core Theory; you are saying that it is wrong."

Carroll, p.356.

"The moral of the fable is that, since an absence of consciousness is conceivably compatible with physical laws, then you can't derive consciousness from those laws to begin with. ...It's important to note that some find the idea of a zombie world immediately conceivable, like Chalmers, while others, like philosopher Dan Dennett, maintain they do not. Personally, I think the latter are lying. Or rather, that deniers purposefully say a zombie world is inconceivable merely to avoid the difficult-to-swallow metaphysical conclusion. ...[T]he z-argument seems to be obviously correct, but then implies the mind and body are 'two separate substances.' And if they are different substances, how can they ever interact? And if they can't interact, how could information pass from one to the other?"

Hoel, *The World Behind the World,* pp.125, 126, 132.

A curious thing about this hypothetical is that in such a world, there would be no way to determine if another person is a zombie. One could only be sure about one's self (unless you are a zombie, in which case, having had no subjective experiences, you would have no way to know that you are missing them).

Carroll goes on, "[a]ccording to poetic naturalism, philosophical zombies are simply inconceivable, **because** 'consciousness' is [only] a particular way of talking about the behavior of certain physical systems. part of a higher-level vocabulary we use to talk about the emergent behavior of the underlying physical system, not something separate from the physical system." *Id.,* p.358 (emphasis added).

Adding, "That doesn't mean it's not real... ."

What does that mean?

Is it part of our physical "reality" or only our mental "reality"?

He says: "I'm suggesting that all of this talk of our inner experiences is a useful way of bundling up the collective behavior of a complex collection of atoms. Individual atoms don't have experiences, but macroscopic agglomerations of them might very well, without invoking any additional ingredients." *Id.*, p.359.

Same question.

As already noted, Carroll fails to confront directly the key role that randomness plays in Darwinian evolution and its implications for determinism. He seems to be asserting that if we were to "turn back the clock" and start over, everything would turn out pretty much the same. As I discussed in *Important Things*, there is significant debate over this question and Carroll's apparent position would be quite an outlier among the experts. Moreover, "pretty much the same" does not seem to be sufficient for his "poetic naturalism."

To be fair, all he claims to be arguing is that the existence of consciousness (and of free will) is not inconsistent with the Core Theory—that these phenomena, if they exist, do not make the Core Theory incorrect.

Well, I agree with that. If something comes into existence that the Core Theory does not anticipate, that does not make the Core Theory wrong—perhaps incomplete, but not incorrect, especially not within its own domain of applicability (as Carroll likes to say). Similarly, the assumption of the correctness of the Core Theory does not imply the non-existence of free will or consciousness. Indeed, the Core Theory is not inconsistent with strong emergence, unless you maintain that there can be nothing more than the elemental particles and the four forces period. (Carroll essentially assumes away strong emergence.) Likewise, despite Carroll's lengthy arguments, establishing the correctness of the Core Theory would not itself prove the non-existence of God.

But, it seems that 470 pages is a lot for such an obvious point.

"A committed reductionist might ... maintain that all causal models should ... include the entire state of the universe.. . Yet there is even a problem with this extreme view—it eliminates the notion of causation entirely. ...[W]hen the entirety of the universe is taken as a whole, there is only exactly what happens, not what can or should have happened (no counterfactuals or interventions), and so causation itself disappears."

Hoel, *The World Behind the World*, p.190 (emphasis added).

CHAPTER 13

"Turtles All the Way Down"?

"[B]ehavior happened because
something that preceded it caused it to happen.
And why did that prior circumstance occur?
Because something that preceded it caused it to happen.
It's antecedent causes [turtles] all the way down... ."

Robert M. Sapolsky
Determined:
A Science of Life without Free Will
(2023)

Freedom—freedom of choice among thoughts and actions—is important to many of us and was at least as or, probably, even more important to many of our ancestors. We are told of the martyrs and heroes who fought, suffered or died for it. Yet, here I am reading about why there is no free will, that is, why all of our actions, decisions and beliefs are just the result of myriad factors over some of which we had only little influence and over most of we had no control. If that is right, do we conclude that freedom just an illusion and the craving for it, just a vulnerability. If so, should not evolution have knocked it out early on? (We would certainly have had fewer historians today.)

In *Determined: A Science of Life without Free Will* (2023), Robert M. Sapolsky uses a large number of examples of empirical studies of brain function and the effects of hormones, coupled with some significant, relatively new research in epigenetics and gene expression (and a lot of description of brain anatomy) to commence his attack on free will.

"[T]he massively trendy field of 'epigenetics,' revealing how early life experience causes long-lasting changes in gene expression in particular brain regions. Now, this is not experience changing genes themselves (*i.e.*, changing DNA sequences), but instead changing their regulation—whether some gene is always active, never active, or active in one context but not another; a lot is known by now about how this works." *Id.*, p.65.

"[O]nly about 5 percent of DNA constitutes genes. The remaining 95 percent? The dizzyingly complex on/off switches, the means by which various environmental influences regulate unique networks of genes, with multiple types of switches on a single gene and multiple genes being regulated by the same type of switch. ...In other words, most DNA is devoted to gene regulation rather than to genes themselves." *Id.*, p.70.

"But—and this is the incredibly important point—put all the scientific results together, from all the relevant scientific disciplines, and there's no room for free will. ...[A]ll these disciplines collectively negate free will because they are all interlinked, constituting the same ultimate body of knowledge." *Id.*, pp.8, 9.

Sapolsky provides a compelling, although rather repetitive, case that the environment and life experiences of your ancestors and yourself influence every thing you do and every firing of each neuron in your brain.

He then argues that to establish free will, one would need to show him an example of a firing of a neuron without **any** such influence.

"Show me a neuron (or brain) whose generation of a behavior is independent of the sum of its biological past, and for the purposes of this book, you've demonstrated free will." *Id.*, p.15.

" [F]ree will can exist only if neurons' actions are completely uninfluenced by all the uncontrollable factors that came before. It's the only requirement there can be, because all that came before, with its varying flavors of uncontrollable luck, is what came to constitute you. This is how you became you." *Id.*, p.84.

"Back, once again, to the show-me scenario—if free will exists, show me a neuron(s) that just caused a behavior to occur in the complete absence of any influences coming from other neurons... ." *Id.*, pp.227-8.

Why he posits such a standard, he does not explain. Even ignoring the utterly random firings which I assume must frequently occur, I find this standard extreme. (If you do not, just skip to the next essay.)

Imagine for a moment the making of a decision completely independently of all prior experience, in a vacuum. How could the alternatives possibly be evaluated; indeed, how could they even be understood?

I very much like dark chocolate; my companion does not like chocolate at all. Our likes and dislikes, whatever their sources, will surely influence or affect our respective decisions whether to eat another Artisanal Chocolate. Does that mean that we do not ourselves choose whether to eat one? Hardly. Does it mean that we do not "freely" choose to eat one? Well, perhaps.

But, really?

I am reminded of a quotation attributed to Abraham Lincoln that I recently read.

"'When I do good I feel good.
When I do bad I feel bad.
And that's my religion.'
—Abraham Lincoln, 1860"

Christopher Reeve
Nothing Is Impossible:Reflections on a New Life
(2002), p.66.

Perhaps, it is a matter of what one thinks the question is.

Do we need to prove that free will exists or prove that it does not exist? For most of us and our predecessors, the question is why and how could it be that we do not have free will. Our minds, our hearts, our emotions and the ways we live all tell us we do. Indeed, it is only science as reflected in determinism that suggests that we don't.

Sapolsky describes computer simulations in which an initial pattern (a row of blocks with some black and some white) are repeatedly transformed pursuant to a fixed set of rules to demonstrate some discoveries of so-called Chaos Theory. It shows that even knowing the specific initial conditions and the rules we may be unable (with our current understanding) to predict the outcome of the process or from knowledge of the outcome and the rules, to identify the initial starting conditions—something we have learned through computers.

"We have a version of the three-body problem, with interactions that are neither linear nor additive. You cannot take a reductive approach, breaking things down to its component parts (the eight different possible trios of boxes and their outcomes), and predict what you're going to get. This is not a system for generating clocks. It's for generating clouds." Sapolsky, *Determined*, p.140.

Sapolsky argues that this fact does not disprove determinism because things can be determined yet be unpredictable. Yes. But, the test is not successfully predicting the outcome the first time but predicting the outcomes of subsequent repetitions of the exercise. If the outcome is determined, then subsequent outcomes can be predicted. They will all be the same, absent some random alteration in some box. If there was a random alteration (or mutation) changing the outcome, then the process was not determined.

I think that the recognition by scientists of the presence of probabilities and the centrality of randomness destroys determinism. You cannot rewind the clock and be assured the same outcome.

"[]he world is filled with instances of indeterministic Brownian motion, with various biological phenomena having evolved to optimally exploit versions of this randomness." *Id.*, p.208.

"[Y]es, Laplacian determinism really does appear to fall apart down at the subatomic level; however, such eensy-weensy indeterminism is vastly unlikely to influence anything about behavior; even if it did, it's even more unlikely that it would produce something resembling free will... ." *Id.*, p.204.

However, the absence of determinism does not establish the presence of free will. So, we look further.

Wait.

What are we looking for? Evidence of free will? But, are we not surrounded by it? We know that we make decisions; we feel like we have choices; indeed, we agonize over many of them. In fact, as Sapolsky acknowledges, "other primates even believe that there is free will." *Id.*, p.6.

The assumption that free will exists permeates our culture, our religions, literature, entertainment. From Eve and the apple, to the Ten Commandments, to Hamlet's soliloquy, to Robert Frost's poem "The Road Not Taken" to a recent Facebook post of a cartoon by a Bill Thinnes showing a road labeled "TRU" with a fork. One branch is "MP"; the other is "TH".

We have choices.

The freedom—no, the necessity—to choose underlies the enormous power of Niko Kazantzakis' novel *The Last Temptation of Christ* (1960). As the author writes in the Prologue:

> "In order to mount the Cross, the summit of sacrifice, and to God, the summit of immateriality, Christ passed through all the stages which the man who struggles passes through. That is why his suffering is so familiar to us; that is why we share it, and why his final victory seems to us so much our own future victory. That part of Christ's nature which was profoundly human helps us... ."

It is not Christ's divinity that is so moving and meaningful to us, but his humanness.

Now, one might quibble over the word" free." How free? Obviously, our decisions are influenced, in varying degrees, by our past, broadly defined, and by our current environment. Indeed, our past and present largely determine the options from among which we will make our choices. No question about that.

The fact that science cannot explain how choice occurs does not mean that it does not exist. It is indisputable that decisions are made. Who or what makes them?

Is Sapolsky claiming that the decisions are all predetermined? (Sean Carroll seems to be saying so. *See* preceding chapter.)

Carroll asserts: "[T]he entirety of both the past and future history are utterly determined by the present." *The Big Picture*, p.32.

The debate about determinism is interesting and somewhat relevant. I would like to know whether if we rewound the clock and let it all start over, we would get the same result, a "somewhat same" result or something new. That would be informative. But, unless we would get exactly the same result, how could the past and the future be all part of the present? (The only way that I can imagine is if all the infinite possible different series of events somehow exist now and always.)

The question of whether we have free will, however, is simply pointless. We live in a world of free will, regardless of what science may say. Even the outspoken anti-free will proponents conclude either that we should live as if we have free will or that, in any event, we cannot help but do so.

"Free will might be an illusion too, But we live in a world which, for all intents and purposes, is indistinguishable from one in which it isn't. So, acting as if we have free will makes operational sense." Krauss, *The Edge of Knowledge,* loc.2985-7.

"Stephen Cave titled a much-discussed June 2016 article in *The Atlantic* 'There's No Such Thing as Free Will . . . but We're Better Off Believing in It Anyway.'"

...

"And thus, perhaps, 'we're better off believing in it anyway.' Truth doesn't always set you free... ."

...

"It is logically indefensible, ludicrous, meaningless to believe that something 'good' can happen to a machine. Nonetheless, I am certain that it is good if people feel less pain and more happiness."

...

"Ninety-nine percent of the time I can't remotely achieve this mindset, but there is nothing to do but try, because it will be freeing."

Sapolsky, *Determined,* pp.387, 392, 403.

I think that the answer is that conscious beings simply occupy a reality different from that of particle physics. Whether our reality will ever be part of a scientific theory of everything is still an open, debatable question.

"I don't understand what consciousness is, can't define it. I can't understand philosophers' writing about it. Or neuroscientists', for that matter... ." *Id.,* p.31.

> "The influential philosopher David Chalmers of New York University weighs in as well, considering that the only thing that comes close to qualifying as a case of strong emergence is consciousness; likewise with another major contributor to this field, Johns Hopkins physicist Sean Carroll, who thinks that while consciousness is the only real reason to be interested in strong emergence, it's sure not a case of it." *Id.*, p.197.

Free will seems to be much like its apparent "sponsor" consciousness. Science cannot explain it, cannot ascertain how it works; yet, we know it exists. It is key to our identities, our self understanding, our social relationships, our cultures. It is silly to contend it does not exist because science has failed to find it.

Note

There are two specific arguments I would like to discuss briefly. First, Sapolsky stresses intent, asserting that intent is determined by things over which we have no control, so, if even if we do make decisions based on intent, that is still not an example of fee will.

> "[W]hile it sure may seem at times that we are free do as we intend, we are never free to intend what we intend. ...[Y]ou don't ultimately control the intent you form. You wish to do something, intend to do it, and then successfully do so. But no matter how fervent, even desperate, you are, you can't successfully wish to wish for a different intent."

Id., pp.19, 46.

I do not think that the emphasis on intent changes the analysis at all.

Second, there is evidence from the monitoring of brain functions that neurons begin taking steps to initiate an action decided on before the subject believes he has made the decision.

> "Thus, three different techniques, monitoring the activity of hundreds of millions of neurons down to single neurons, all show that at the moment when we believe that we are consciously and freely choosing to do something, the neuro-biological die has already been cast."

Id., p.24.

Does this mean that the decision was predetermined and the frontal cortex simply constructs an illusion of decision-making to justify the predetermined outcome? That seems quite unlikely; although, there are experiments in which it appears that something like that appears to occur. I note that Sapolsky concludes that this set of evidence is not relevant to the question: "I think all that can be concluded is that in some fairly artificial circumstances, certain measures of brain function are moderately predictive of a subsequent behavior. ...I think that is irrelevant." *Id.*, p.36. I also observe that some elaborate system of fabricating explanations in order to create a false belief that one's actions are volitional does not seem to be very adaptive, so it would not likely to arise through evolution.

Sapolsky asks rhetorically: "How do we get from randomness to rationality?" *Id.*, p.229. Hmmm. How do we get from no free will to rationality?

Consciousness

CHAPTER 14

Dialogues

I recently discovered that I was mistaken when I wrote in *Important Things We Don't Know* (p.492, n18) that the theories of Julian Jaynes had faded away after the publication of his (only) book, *The Origin of Consciousness in the Breakdown of the Bicameral Mind*, in 1976.

In fact, the book was reissued in 1990, with a substantial and substantive afterword by Jaynes. Following his death in 1997, the Julian Jaynes Society was formed. It is still active and has sponsored the publication of several books about his theories. A new release of Jaynes' book occurred in 2000. And, there seems to be an increased interest in recent years based on the number of articles in the journal *Frontiers in Psychology*. Erik Hoel calls it "a cult classic." *The World Behind the World: Consciousness, Free Will, and the Limits of Science* (2023), p.9.

I read Julian Jaynes' *The Origin of Consciousness*, shortly after it was originally published. It prompted me then to read *The Iliad*. I was impressed by how apt Jaynes' description of the warriors was: "They were noble automatons who knew not what they did." *Id.* (2000 edition), p.75. It was eerie, actually. A world so foreign, not quite human.

(Otherwise, I had no opinion about the "bicameral mind," having had no experience with gods speaking in my head.)

But, his concept of consciousness, what he was interested in investigating, resonated with me. It was what I wanted to know about: not simple sentience nor even cognition, but how we internally respond to things, how we experience:

> "this constant companion of hosts of associations, hopes, fears, affections, knowledges, colors, smells, toothaches, thrills, tickles, pleasures, distresses, and desires—**where and how in evolution could all this wonderful tapestry of inner experience have evolved? How can we derive this inwardness out of mere matter?**"

Id., p.3 (emphasis added).

"Alfred Russel Wallace [the co-discoverer of natural selection] felt the evidence showed that some metaphysical force had directed evolution at three different points: the beginning of life, the beginning of consciousness, and the beginning of civilized culture." *Id.*, pp.9-10.

Jaynes wrote: "Subjective conscious mind ... allows us to shortcut behavioral processes and arrive at more adequate decisions. Like mathematics, it is an operator rather than a thing or repository. And it is intimately bound up with volition and decision." *Id.*, p.55.

"It is important to notice how Jaynes defines consciousness. It has nothing to do with perception or sensation. ...For example, the 'conscious experience' of a bright color red, or a sharp pain. These examples of subjective experience, that fascinating aspect of our mental life, is not what Jaynes wants to explain. [H]e is searching for another holy grail: how is it possible that we can pose these kinds of questions at all?"

erikweijers,"Summary of the Origin of Consciousness," posted 29 September 2014.

The other thing that I found relevant to my own experience was his concept of internal dialogues between the two hemispheres of our brain. But, in fact, I now realize he did not so say.

I have reread the book now.

I.

The controversial aspect of his theory was the proposition that his form of consciousness arose only about 3500 years ago, between the writing of *The Iliad* (estimated as between 1230 BC and 850 BC) and the writing of *The Odyssey*, at least a century later. Jaynes attributes the change to societal crises that demanded a new approach. Belief in the gods was eroded by the traumatic events of the time, and a new way of thinking about the world and humankind's role in it emerged with the breakdown of the bicameral mind. Say, 3,000 years ago. Yet, human burial practices date back perhaps 100,000 years, artistic expression had existed for well in excess of 35,000 years and language for, perhaps, as much as 50,000 years. "For if consciousness is based on language, then it follows that it is of a much more recent origin than has heretofore been supposed. Consciousness comes after language!" Jaynes, *The Origin of Consciousness*, p.66.

Jaynes presents pretty compelling evidence from ancient literature, architecture and art that sometime around 1000 BC the human mind changed dramatically. Whether you call it the origin of consciousness or of a new theory of the mind or something else; it represents the emergence of modern humankind. Two questions jump out. First, did it occur everywhere? Second, were the changes and results the same in all cases? If the answers are yes, then how could that happen? Perhaps, there were initially many differences and homogeneity arose through natural selection? But, there was simply not enough time. Cultural evolution occurs far, far more rapidly than biological evolution, but we are talking about the whole world.

"What is interesting to me in this speculation is the possibility that as consciousness develops, it can develop in slightly different ways..." *Id.*,p.252.

In response,

"...[C]ritics have consistently pointed out two things. The first is that beyond the textual analysis the book contains no actual evidence that people were not conscious prior to the Homeric age... . The second issue ... is that there is an eminently more sensible interpretation of the textual evidence Jaynes presents, which is that it is our understanding of consciousness that has evolved since ancient times. Consciousness was not absent in ancient Greece, but rather, at least broadly speaking, that is around the time in history when a more detailed understanding of consciousness began to develop and find its way into text."

Erik Hoel, *The World Behind the World* pp.10 -11.

"The extent and vibrancy of the formulations and reformulations of philosophy, religion and behaviours from the eighth to the third centuries bc in the Yellow and Yangtze River valleys, the eastern Mediterranean, the Levant and the Ganges Valley have been much remarked on, [a time] when humanity was taking 'a deep breath' and pondering profound questions that stimulated new levels of consciousness... . Other scholars have followed suit... . ...Not all are convinced by the argument of multiple simultaneous watersheds during which archaic values were abandoned or modernised, ... noting that some of the apparent transformations took place hundreds, or even thousands of years before the supposed 'age' of change."

Peter Frankopan, *The Earth Transformed: An Untold History* (2023), pp.151, 152.

Yet,

"[S]omething did develop, which is our ability to access more and more of our phenomenal consciousness. That is, the development of the intrinsic perspective was the process of evolving our language and concepts such that the richness of access consciousness began to approach the richness of phenomenal consciousness, which is the situation we find ourselves in today...[,] what the ancient Egyptians ..., at least if we judge by their literature, seemed to lack—access to the depths of their own consciousness."

Hoel, *The World Behind the World*, p.18.

"[O]ur experience (phenomenal consciousness, what it is like to be us) outstrips in complexity our ability to express it (the parts of our consciousness we can express). ...A novel eschews all such extrinsic trappings. Not meant to be performed, it is merely words on the page, meant to be read in privacy—this, perhaps, made it inevitable it would become the purest expression of the intrinsic perspective. Novels, however, take place in an imaginary world where the problem of other minds does not exist, where mental states, like rage or ennui, can be referred to as directly as one does tables and chairs. ...No other medium can mimic this ability. Which actually provides a continued justification of the novel as an artform."

...

"Humans, by finding our depths, learned to dramatize our internal lives through literature, and in doing so we learned how to make the mundane extraordinary."

Id., pp.18, 31, 32.

"Consciousness was a verboten scientific subject for most of the twentieth century. ...All the way to the 1990s, research into consciousness was not viewed as 'proper' science." *Id.*, pp.68, 69.

"The reason neuroscience is a quagmire is that it ignores the brain's entire evolved purpose, it's very *raison d'être*—maintaining a stream of consciousness. Every region or module operates on and requires the stream of consciousness in order to make sensible decisions—consciousness is like a brain-wide frame of reference for every other cognitive function. It is the elephant in the brain that neuroscientists feel only parts of, blindly. To make minds manageable, neuroscience has minimized the importance of consciousness... ."

Id., pp.64, 65.

"[I]t will eventually become clear that nothing in the brain makes sense except in the light of consciousness." *Id.*, p.68.

II.

Jaynes describes experiments conducted by psychologists that appear rather convincingly to demonstrate that consciousness is not an integral part of many mental capabilities. For example, playing a musical instrument is not a conscious action apart from the decision to do so and the choice of what to play. The same is true for speaking and writing. In these activities, consciousness would be an impediment to performance. Likewise, consciousness is not necessary for learning. It is not necessary for thinking or solving problems. (Whereas, 'thinking about", or "thinking of", something is an act of consciousness.) ("What seemed to be happening was that thinking was automatic and not really conscious once a stimulus word had been given, and, previous to that, the particular type of association demanded had been adequately understood by the observer." Jaynes, *The Origin of Consciousness*, p.39.

The making of judgments (which object is heavier based on lifting them, which one is taller or prettier based on visual inspection, which thing is more important) is not an act of consciousness. Consciousness is similarly not required for reasoning or insight or understanding; "consciousness is indeed like a helpless spectator, having little to do." *Id.*, p.33. There are numerous incidents of scientists reporting how the answer or the idea just came to them in a dream, while shaving or showering, on a walk. "Indeed, it is sometimes almost as if the problem had to be forgotten to be solved." *Id.*, p.44.

"So we arrive at the position that the actual process of thinking, so usually thought to be the very life of consciousness, is not conscious at all and that only its preparation, its materials, and its end result are consciously perceived."

...

"[T]here are several stages of creative thought: first, a stage of preparation in which the problem is consciously worked over; then a period of incubation without any conscious concentration upon the problem; and then the illumination which is later justified by logic."

Id., pp.41, 44.

This conclusion is rather remarkable.

It makes irrelevant much of what we say about consciousness. "Consciousness is a much smaller part of our mental life than we are conscious of, because we cannot be conscious of what we are not conscious of." *Id.*, p.23. Moreover, "[I]t is perfectly possible that there could have existed a race of men who spoke, judged, reasoned, solved problems, indeed did most of the things that we do, but who were not conscious at all." *Id.*, p.46. "[A] civilization without consciousness is possible...." *Id.*, p.47.

David Chalmers' zombies?

III.

Jaynes described how the characters in *The Iliad* acted apparently without will or volition.

One commentator focused on volition as key to Jaynes' concept of consciousness.

> "According to Jaynes, prior to the emergence of consciousness, the human mind was bicameral, *i.e.*, it was split into two parts: a decision-making part and a follower part. Importantly, neither one of these separate parts was conscious. "
>
> ...
>
> "For Jaynes, the absence of consciousness is actually marked by an absence of self-volition. Bicameral people did not feel they were responsible for their decisions and actions, and this is because they were not conscious. The apparent causal agents in human affairs were not humans but gods."

James W. Moore, "Volition in Jaynes' *The Origin of Consciousness … ,*" *Frontiers in Psychology,* December 20, 2021 (National Library of Medicine).

I think that the word "volition" is inadequate here. We need something more all-encompassing. The trendy term today is "agency". They lacked agency; consciousness brought with it agency: awareness of choice, of decisions; a feeling of responsibility for one's actions and for their consequences; the experience of being a "player." Consciousness creates narratives, with "me" generally at the center. It allows one to imagine and play out different scenarios, assessing their various outcomes, to plan and to strategize. And, permits the emergence of treachery and strategic deception.

IV.

Jaynes described language as primarily metaphor. New words are introduced through metaphor. Objects used as metaphors often have associated qualities or characteristics which can become attributed to the new word or idea that the metaphor is being used to illuminate. Thus, language expands, as does what language can express.

Maybe, that is right, but Jaynes then goes on to assert that consciousness, based on language, also consists of metaphor. ("Consciousness is not all language, but it is generated by it and accessed by it." Jaynes, *The Origin of Consciousness*, p.449. Or, "Subjective consciousness... is... the development on the basis of linguistic metaphors of an operation space in which an 'I' could narratize out alternative actions to their consequences... ." *Id.*, p.236.)

That feels inadequate. Something more seems to be happening. Certainly, we developed a linear concept of time. (Jaynes says we "spacialized" time, but it appears to me to be more one dimensional than three: "You cannot, absolutely cannot think of time except by spatializing it. Consciousness is always a spatialization in which the diachronic is turned into the synchronic, in which what has happened in time is excerpted and seen in side-by-sideness. *Id.*, p.60.) And, we also came to create narratives in our minds, generally with an image of ourselves at the center. "The assigning of causes to our behavior or saying why we did a particular thing is all a part of narratization. Consciousness is ever ready to explain anything we happen to find ourselves doing." *Id.*, p.64. We also talk to ourselves; although, Jaynes does not write about that.

I find his theory that extreme stress and the need to adapt to new challenges underlay the changes in the way we think to be highly plausible conceptually and historically. The bicameral mind, however, is only an inference drawn to enable a theory of a breakdown. He has no evidence that one physically distinct part of the brain handled the routine things while another part made the decisions and issued commands. If that is how the mind functioned after language arose, then it seems quite plausible that the commands were experienced as the voices of the gods.

V.

I also failed to grasp his concept of the bicameral mind as a mechanism of social organization and control. ("The bicameral mind is a form of social control and it is that form of social control which allowed mankind to move from small hunter-gatherer groups to large agricultural communities. *Id.*, p.126.) Perhaps, all he meant was that people all tended to think alike and were less greedy than modern man.

"In the bicameral era, the bicameral mind was the social control, not fear or repression or even law. There were no private ambitions, no private grudges, no private frustrations, no private anything, since bicameral men had no internal 'space' in which to be private, and no analog 'I' to be private with. **Within each bicameral state, therefore, the people were probably more peaceful and friendly than in any civilization since.** ...But at the interfaces between different bicameral civilizations, the problems were complex and quite different."

Id., p.205 (emphasis added).

Yet, he offered no explanation of the emergence of private property, of the appearance of kings and priests or of the creation of societal structures and hierarchies, even though all of that happened during the era of the bicameral mind. Things may have gotten much bloodier after the "breakdown," but only as a matter of degree.

VI.

How did I come to have such a clear but erroneous recollection of Jaynes' theory?

Well, there are some clues.

First, although, Jaynes's theory of the bicameral mind is about two parts of the mind, not the brain; he devoted a lot of attention to the two hemispheres of the brain. The reader could easily confuse the two topics. Indeed, in his 1990 Afterword, Jaynes noted: "The two hemispheres of the brain are not the bicameral mind but its present neurological model." Jaynes, *The Origin of Consciousness*, p. 456. That statement does not really clarify the matter.

Second, Jaynes stresses the apparent independence and language abilities of the two hemispheres of the human brain. He references numerous clinical studies that seem to establish that the two hemispheres of the human brain operate independently; that both hemispheres understand language, while only one can control our speech; and that there is very substantial redundancy within and between the hemispheres.

"The situation then is one where the areas on the right hemisphere that correspond to the speech areas have seemingly no easily observable major function. Could it be that these silent 'speech' areas on the right hemisphere had some function at an earlier stage in man's history that now they do not have?"

...

"[I]s it possible to think of the two hemispheres of the brain almost as two individuals, only one of which can overtly speak, while both can listen and both understand?"

...

"[T]he studies , these commissurotomy patients demonstrate conclusively that the two hemispheres can function so as to seem like two independent persons... ."

Id., pp.103, 113, 117.

Third, Jaynes hypothesizing three means by which consciousness could have arise: the recognition that other people are separate selves with their own perspectives; the survival need for deception and the realization that their gods had disappeared, leading to the impulse to pray.

"It is ... a possibility that before an individual man had an interior self, he unconsciously first posited it in others... ." *Id.*, p.219.

"Deceit may also be a cause of consciousness. ...[T]he kind of deceit that is treachery is quite another matter. It is impossible for an animal or for a bicameral man. Long-term deceit requires the invention of an analog self that can 'do' or 'be' something quite different from what the person actually does or is, as seen by his associates. ...It is an easy matter to imagine how important for survival during these centuries such an ability would be." *Id.*, p.219.

"My god has forsaken me and disappeared... . This is *de facto* the breakdown of the bicameral mind." *Id.*, p.225.

"What then takes over their function? How is action initiated? If hallucinated voices are no longer adequate to the escalating complexities of behavior, how can decisions be made?" *Id.*, p.236

All of these circumstances demand dialogue and consultation. So, perhaps it occurred within ourselves.

I suspect that those are the connections my mind made in the late 1970s.

We should note again that Jaynes used a very restrictive concept of consciousness. In his 1990 Afterword, he stresses that point:

> "[C]areful distinctions have been made between what is intro-spectable and all the hosts of other neural abilities we have come to call cognition." *Id.*, p.447.

> "The most common error which I did not emphasize sufficiently is to confuse consciousness with perception. Perception is sensing a stimulus and responding appropriately. And this can happen on a nonconscious level... ." *Id.*, p.448.

I think he goes too far in asserting that when one sees a table and says" I see a table," consciousness is not involved. I can see that, in a limited sense, there could be perception without consciousness, but when one notices (takes note of) something, consciousness is clearly involved. Similarly, when one expresses a judgment ("I see a pretty woman"). The judgment may have been unconscious, but the expression of it is not.

Consciousness is the exercise of introspection, of consideration or deliberation. It is self awareness, the recognition that one is a "self," distinct from other "selves".

> "Self-awareness usually means the consciousness of our own persona over time, a sense of who we are, our hopes and fears, as we daydream about ourselves in relation to others. The animal is not shown to be imagining himself anywhere else, or thinking of his life over time, or introspecting in any sense—all signs of a conscious self."

Id., p.460.

CHAPTER 15

Voice of the Unconscious

Reading about the planned release of two new books by Cormac McCarthy in the fall of 2022, I saw reference to his first nonfiction publication, which was in *Nautilus* in 2017, entitled "The Kekulé Problem: Where did language come from?" So I read it. It caused me to realize that in *Important Things,* I had not given enough attention to the nature and role of language or to the nature and role of the unconscious mind.

In June 2023, I read his two new, and last, books—*The Passenger* and *Stella Maris*. Remarkable. The set is a true *tour d' force*. To my delight, they further explore the themes of his 2017 non-fiction article and related subjects. The characters—Bobby, a good theoretical physicist turned salvage diver, and his beautiful sister, a highly gifted mathematician institutionalized because of hallucinations—discuss and expound on these matters, variously, flippantly, sardonically, ironically. Marvelous. So, in this essay (and some other essays in this second edition), I quote several of the memorable passages.

LANGUAGE

"Reflective consciousness ...
transforms communication into language... ."

John Hands
Cosmosapiens:
Human Evolution from the Origin of the Universe
(2015), p.448.

Undoubtedly one of the most significant and unique traits of human beings. I am referring to more than a shared association of a particular sound with a particular type of object, of a type of danger or a food, even of a particular feeling. In such examples, sounds made are just a kind of body language addressed to the ears rather than the eyes, just as odors address the nose. All are forms of communication used by all animals. But, language? What distinguishes language?

Language does not require speech. It can be accomplished through signs or even signals. With language, words can convey abstract concepts and present narratives. Language can describe the past, the future, hopes and ideas. Perhaps most importantly, language enables exchanges, conversation, give and take.. Only humans tell stories, create narratives and converse.

Language enables the transmission of information and ideas, of observations and speculation. As a result, it enables the collective accumulation of vast quantities of knowledge. Just visit any large library and look around. It also has aesthetic value in itself. Good writing does not just communicate ideas, but also feelings, emotions. The sound can be like music.

"Music is made out of nothing but some fairly simple rules. Yet it's true that no one made them up. The rules. The notes themselves amount to almost nothing. But why some particular arrangement of these notes should have such a profound effect on our emotions is a mystery beyond even the hope of comprehension. Music is not a language. It has no reference to anything other than itself."

Cormac McCarthy, *Stella Maris* (2022), p.38.

Language also contributes to memory.

"Young children can certainly form memories, but these fade as they age into their teens. Traumatic memories from physical, emotional, or sexual abuse leave deep albeit unconscious traces in the mind. But explicit, pellucid memories of your toddler years are forever lost in time. ...[T]oday's psychologists attribute this amnesia to the dual absence of language and abstract thought. As those cognitive processes mature, so does your ability to lay down and recall explicit memories, marking the emergence of an autobiographical self."

Christof Koch, *Then I Am Myself the World: What Consciousness Is and How to Expand It* (2024), p.24.

The origin or emergence of language is impossible to pinpoint or even to investigate. Language leaves no footprints. It has no physical manifestation until the subsequent development of writing. We may find evidence of the physical faculties that could enable speech or of anatomical changes that might have arisen because greater facility to speak had adaptation value. But, that is it.

There is indirect evidence, however.

> "It ... seems reasonable to hypothesize that painted or engraved symbols were paralleled by speech, however basic, that subsequently developed more sophistication. ...[P]articular achievements, like a group of humans migrating across 100 kilometres of ocean or trading in goods, require speech. Although the evidence of language in prehistoric times is necessarily indirect, it suggests that spoken language emerged in the Upper Palaeolithic."

Hands, *Cosmosapiens*, p.449.

Presumably, the appearance of language followed the development of some level of consciousness (for which we have no explanation, either) and probably after the beginnings of artistic expression. So, we can guess that it began to emerge some 50,000 years ago.

> "[T]hought is much older than language. Human language is probably tens of thousands of years old, but it is difficult to believe that before language our ancestors did not think—or that animals, or human infants who do not talk yet, do not carry out some form of thinking... ."

Giorgio Parisi, *In a Flight of Starlings: The Wonders of Complex Systems* (2023), p.103.

> "If early man, through these two million years, had even a primordial speech, why is there so little evidence of even simple culture or technology? For there is precious little archaeologically up to 40,000 B.C., other than the crudest of stone tools.

...

"It is, I suggest, as late as the Mesolithic era, about 10,000 B.C. to 8000 B.C. when names first occurred. ...[L]iving is characterized by a much greater stability of population, rather than the necessary mobility of the hunting groups which preceded them with their large mortality. ...[I]t is not difficult to see both the need and the likelihood of a carry-over of nouns into names for individual persons."

Julian Jaynes, *The Origin of Consciousness in the Breakdown of the Bicameral Mind* (1976)(2000 edition), pp.130, 135-6.

"What additional developments then pushed hominids to a level where the recognition of those goals could be internalized, giving the organism a distinct sense of existence within that environment, allowing it to be both subject and object in decision-making? One possibility is the evolutionary emergence of language. ...[I]t is virtually impossible to imagine constructing thoughts without the generative processes of language. ...One doesn't know what one's thoughts are until they are formulated by language. ...The neurologist and writer Oliver Sacks wrote, 'It is through inner speech that the child develops his own concepts and meaning; it is through inner speech that he achieves his own identity.' ...[W]ithout language, there literally is no mind, just a brain."

Lawrence M. Krauss, The Edge of Knowledge: Unsolved Mysteries of the Cosmos (2023) (Kindle), loc.2922-36.

"Self-awareness and silent, inner speech develop much later. Just like dreaming, these are complex cognitive processes linked to linguistic processing that take years to mature... ." Koch, p.32.

One view is that language arose only once and then spread rapidly throughout human communities, because all known languages have similar structure. Perhaps, however, it appeared in several places, but maybe not entirely independently. There is no reason to think that it was the result of a genetic mutation or physical change. (There appears to be a relatively new gene—maybe about 100,000 years old—that seems to facilitate speech, which is a different matter.) Communication could well have developed from body language to sign language to speech. However, there must have been some predisposition existing in humans at the time.*

"The extraordinary usefulness of language turned it into an overnight epidemic. It seems to have spread to every remote pocket of humanity almost instantly."

...

"But you have to understand what the advent of language was like. The brain had done pretty well without it for quite a few million years. The arrival of language was like the invasion of a parasitic system. Co-opting those areas of the brain that were the least dedicated. The most susceptible to appropriation."

...

"...[T]he unconscious system of guidance is millions of years old, speech less than a hundred thousand. The brain had no idea any of this was coming. The unconscious must have had to do all sorts of scrambling around to accommodate a system that proved perfectly relentless."

McCarthy, *Stella Maris*, pp.174, 173, 174.

THE UNCONSCIOUS

Modern humans perceive that they think using language. We rehearse, debate, even fantasize using words in our heads, talking to ourselves. We even often have language as part of our dreams. Of course, we need our thoughts to be in language in order to communicate them. But, is that how they are formed?

We find it difficult to contemplate thinking without the use of language, but consider some commonplace occurrences. Have you ever said, "I can't find the words to express it"? Or, felt as if "a light went on" in your head when you suddenly understood something? What about solving problems in your sleep ("Let me sleep on it") ? There are people who sleep with a notepad next to them to record ideas that come to them in their sleep. And, there are well-publicized claims of mathematical problems being solved while sleeping.

"[B]y 1875 most psychologists were insisting that consciousness was but a small part of mental life, and that unconscious sensations, unconscious ideas, and unconscious judgments made up the majority of mental processes." Jaynes, *The Origin of Consciousness*, p.3.

The title of McCarthy's article mentioned above is a reference to such an example, a dream of a snake with its tail in its mouth, forming a circle, causing the nineteenth century German scientist Friedrich August Kekulé to realize that the configuration of the benzene molecule is a ring. But, is this a case, as McCarthy argues, of the unconscious mind sending the answer in the form of an image or of the unconscious (or conscious) mind recognizing the answer in an image coincidentally appearing?

The answer does not much matter for my purposes here. The point is that much of our "thinking" occurs without our awareness, that is, outside of our consciousness.

'[S]ome psychologists argue that much of thinking is carried out unconsciously; what is consciously accessible are the projections of these thoughts onto the visual, auditory, or linguistic processing machinery in the brain." Koch, p.39.

DREAMS

As to dreams, are they the mere rearrangement and disgorgement of the stuff stored in our subconscious, derived from our sensory facilities?

Or, are they more, as Nick Bottom says in Act IV of Shakespeare's *Midsummer's Night Dream?*

> "I have had a most rare vision.
> I have had a dream
> past the wit of man
> to say what dream it was.
> ...
> "The eye of man hath not heard,
> the ear of man hath not seen,
> man's hand is not able to taste,
> his tongue to conceive,
> nor his heart to report
> what my dream was."

(I thank my college classmate Dick Kellogg for bringing this soliloquy to my attention, in a totally different context.)

I have frequent dreams that are a jumble of recognizable images and excerpts of experienced events making little sense. But, I also have dreams of two types that are quite different. The first is a repeating creation of an imagined place and landscape, complete with an understanding of a map of the location so that I can find my way back on subsequent nights. In some, the central feature consists of a dramatic natural vista; in some, an interesting building, including the interiors;

in some, a setting with buildings and natural features. In successive dreams, I will revisit and continue to explore these places until they return no more. The other odd type is the dream in which I make a lengthy presentation or speech. Occasionally, the setting returns a night or two later for me to continue. The contents of what I say are surprisingly coherent and often actually insightful. And, these dreams are not the reliving of past "glories." I could only wish.

"I suppose that sometimes the unconscious will keep working on certain dreams, revising them, hoping you'll get it. That's not the interesting part though. The interesting part is that it knows that you havent gotten it. It doesnt really have anything to go on. It's a mind reader? ...[P]eople dont have dreams that they're not in. People are interested in other people. But your unconscious is not. Or only as they might directly affect you. It's been hired to do a very specific job. It never sleeps. It's more faithful than God."

McCarthy, *Stella Maris*, p.79.

"Dreams feel as real as life—the primary distinction between dreaming and waking consciousness is an absence of a sense of self, insight, self-reflection. You aren't surprised that you can fly, walk through walls, or meet long-dead animal companions, lovers, parents, or siblings. You are along for the ride, watching a movie that someone else is directing. Some sleepers do, on occasion, 'wake up' inside their dream, realize that they are dreaming, and take limited control of events, becoming their own 'dream director.'"

Koch, p.46.

So, the one type of dream is mainly visual images, but in a realistic, logical and manipulatable arrangement, like a video game. The other type is essentially verbal, constructed mainly of words. And, they both reflect the input of imagination and of intelligence or logical thinking. How can that happen in the subconscious?

> Similarly, "[I]f a psychosis was just some synapses misfiring why wouldn't you simply get static? But you dont. You get a carefully crafted and fairly articulate world never seen before. Who's doing this?" McCarthy, *Stella Maris*, p.51.

And, what about "near death" or "temporary death" experiences? The reports say that one's life "flashes before your eyes." Sometimes, one apparently observes and overhears what is going on around them.Maybe even sees one's own body. And, some survivors say that they find themselves in a new, unfamiliar place. How does this kind of thing happen?

The wonder is not that it happens or, even, whether it happens, but that it is recognized and remembered.

THE SUBCONSCIOUS

This interplay between the subconscious and consciousness is quite remarkable.

The cognitive process is apparently independent of language, and it largely occurs in our unconscious or subconscious mind. Now, I am not interested here in Freud's theory of repressed mental content. I use "unconscious" just in the sense of unaware and not intentional. And, I am not talking about the more primitive part of the brain that operates our bodies.**

Humans, at least, appear to have additional, extremely important unconscious capabilities, including imagination, creativity and cognitive abilities like mathematics and problem solving. (Do these capacities exist in other mammals or in other life forms?) And, the unconscious "learns" with experience. We learn to ride a bike, to swim, to drive a car, to speak different languages. Some people even become superb musicians; others, world class athletes.

David Brooks quotes the neuropsychologist Elkhonon Goldberg as observing:

> "'Frequently, when I am faced with what would appear from the outside to be a challenging problem, the grinding mental computation is somehow circumvented, rendered, as if by magic, unnecessary. The solution comes effortlessly, seamlessly, seemingly by itself. What I have lost with age in my capacity for hard mental work, I seem to have gained in my capacity for instantaneous, almost unfairly easy insight.'"

The Second Mountain (2019), p.128.

"Then there is a period of incubation in which the problem is abandoned, at least consciously. This incubation ends suddenly with a moment of illumination, which often occurs in a situation unrelated to the problem you're trying to solve. ...In the end, after the illumination provides the general way to tackle the problem, the solution must actually be formulated. ...It is a very interesting description of the process, and one that assigns a prominent role to unconscious thinking."

Parisi, *In a Flight of Starlings*, pp.98-9.

And, what about prodigies? Just very fast learners?

According to a Noble prize winning physicist, "[p]sychophysics reveals that consciousness does not direct most actions, but instead processes reports of them, from unconscious units that do the work."

Frank Wilczek. *Fundamentals: Ten Keys to Reality* (2021), p.xvii. "Humans themselves know many things that are not available to human consciousness, such as how to process visual information at incredible speeds, or how to make their bodies stay upright, walk, and run." *Id.,* p.205.

And, from a contemporary Chinese science fiction writer:

> "[T]he human brain was to some extent a problem-solving machine. ...Much of the process didn't require the participation of consciousness. Many important cognitive tasks were carried out subconsciously, with consciousness only providing supplemental functions like monitoring, storing, organizing, and refining."

Baoshu, *The Redemption of Time* (2016), p.51.

Yet, Giorgio Parisi writes:

> "We have the impression of thinking using words, formulating sentences. This is the case not just when we talk to others, but also when we reflect in silence....If someone asked us to reflect on a problem without using words, we would feel completely helpless: we are not capable of solving problems in our heads without formalizing or embodying our reasoning in words... . ...The way in which we think, however, is not completely based on words. In fact, when we begin to think or say a sentence, we need to know where we are headed. The whole sentence must be present in our mind in nonverbal form before it is expressed in words."

In a Flight of Starlings, pp.101-2.

How does the unconscious do these things? Not with words or through internal dialogue. That is how we organize, flesh out and make accessible the output of the thinking process. I rehearse the words before writing them. As Einstein reportedly said: "A new idea comes suddenly and in a rather intuitive way. That means it is not reached by conscious logical conclusions." So, how do we think? How does it happen? We just do not know.

"Talking is just recording what you're thinking. It's not the thing itself. When I'm talking to you some separate part of my mind is composing what I'm about to say. But it's not yet in the form of words. So what is it in the form of? ...Aside from raising the spectre of an infinite regress—as in who is whispering to the whisperer—it raises the question of a language of thought." McCarthy, *Stella Maris*, p.28.

In addition, we do not know how the unconscious knows the questions or how it communicates the answers to the conscious mind—neither how either one "speaks" nor how the other "hears." From my chair (wheelchair), I conclude that thinking must have preceded language, but how then did the unconscious and conscious mind operate without language?

"But if incubation, whether for small matters or large, is an unconscious process, we then have to ask ourselves what kind of logic it follows and how it comes about. Very often we take for granted that thought is verbal and that unconscious reasoning is not. ...Einstein would not have agreed, arguing that being fully conscious is one end of a spectrum that is never actually reached: there is always, in all thinking, an admixture of the unconscious."

Parisi, *In a Flight of Starlings*, pp.101.

"Unfortunately it is quite difficult to understand what type of logic nonverbal thinking follows, not least because logic refers to language, and it is almost impossible to study a nonverbal thought using the tools of language." *Id.*, p.103.

The unconscious process in mysterious and extremely powerful. "By one calculation the mind can take in eleven million bits of information a second, of which the conscious mind is aware of forty. ... As Timothy Wilson of the University of Virginia put it, consciousness is like a snowball sitting on an iceberg. In other words, most of what guides us is not our conscious rationalization; it's our unconscious realm." Brooks, *The Second Mountain*, p.113.

AND,

It is clear that language opened vast opportunities for human social and intellectual interactions. But, is it also possible that the subsequent preeminence of language has imposed limitations on human beings by separating us from, or stifling, the voice of our unconscious? ***

"[T]he advent of language, aside from the enormous value of it, was disruptive. Very disruptive. Of a piece with its value. Creative destruction. All sorts of talents and skills must have been lost. Mostly communicative. But also things like navigation and probably even the richness of dreams. ... . In the end this strange new code must have replaced at least part of the world with what can be said about it. Reality with opinion. Narrative with commentary."

McCarthy, *Stella Maris*, p.175.

Is there a world we are missing because it is neither expressed nor, perhaps, expressible in language?

Because,

"[m]any things are happening simultaneously within our brains, but our natural consciousness only allows us to attend to one at a time, and much is hidden from it altogether. As our ability to monitor and interpret brain state improve, it will be possible to present our inner selves to our perceiving self through our visual system, on displays, bypassing the filter of natural consciousness."

Frank Wilczek, *Fundamentals: Ten Keys to Reality* (2021), pp.185-6.

There are reasons to believe, and many hints to us, that the un-conscious mind has potentials we can hardly imagine. ****

ENDNOTES

* Writing appeared only about 3,000-5,000 years ago, depending on what one considers to be writing. "Most linguistics scholars consider the earliest writing systems were cuneiform engraved on clay tablets from around 5,000 years ago in Sumer, Mesopotamia and Egyptian hieroglyphs engraved on stone from roughly the same period. ...Writing was invented independently in China, where the earliest evidence so far discovered consists of inscriptions on cattle shoulder-blades and tortoise shells used in divination rituals dating from around 1250 BCE in the Shang dynasty." Hands, *Cosmosapiens*, pp.449, 472.

** "The vertebrate peripheral nervous system is divided into two. The autonomic nervous system comprises motor nerve fibres signalling to internal effector organs like the heart, lungs, and endocrine glands (which produce and secrete chemicals known as hormones into the blood circulation system to distant target cells where they regulate cellular metabolism) principally to maintain homeostasis, or regular functioning of the adult animal. It is regulated by the most ancient part of the central nervous system, the brain stem (which humans share with descendants of the earliest reptiles) responding automatically to stimuli. The somatic nervous system comprises motor nerve fibres signalling to effector organs, like muscles, principally on or near the outer layers of the animal; it is activated by the central nervous system responding to external, sensory stimuli and is under voluntary control." Hands, *Cosmosapiens*, pp.400-401.

*** "What deadens us most to God's presence within us, I think, is the inner dialogue that we are continuously engaged in with ourselves, the endless chatter of human thought." Frederick Buechner, *Telling Secrets* (1991), p.105.

**** "The Greeks had a concept, later seized by Goethe, called the daemonic. A daemon is a calling, an obsession, a source of lasting and sometimes manic energy. Daemons are mysterious clusters of energy deep in the unconscious that were charged by some mysterious event in childhood that we imperfectly comprehend—or by some experience of trauma, or by some great love or joy or longing... ." Brooks, *The Second Mountain*, p.111.

CHAPTER 16

Sentience

"'The question is not, Can they reason?
nor, Can they talk?
but, Can they suffer?'"

Jeremy Bentham
Introduction to the Principles of Morals and Legislation
(1789), Ch 17, n.122
Quoted by Nicholas Humphrey

A new book by neuropsychologist Nicholas Humphrey, *Sentience: The Invention of Consciousness* (2023), discusses the significance and potential sources of sentience or phenomenal consciousness (in contrast to cognitive consciousness). "Phenomenal consciousness is unquestionably a variety of consciousness. We know about our sensations. They influence our judgements and decisions. But, compared to other mental states of which we're conscious, sensations are clearly in a class of their own." *Id.*, p.3.

"[Psychologists] call this special quality 'phenomenal quality', and they call particular examples of it—such as phenomenal redness or phenomenal

---

---

sweetness—'qualia'. Moreover, they say that, when we experience qualia, 'it's like something' to have the experience: it's like something to feel the pain of a bee sting, When we are aware of having experiences with phenomenal qualities, we can be said to be 'phenomenally conscious'." *Id.*, p.3.

Humphrey starts with the assumption (or presumption) that consciousness arose through natural selection. Thus, the constituent elements in order to have evolved must have had an impact on the behavior or characteristics of organisms **and** those impacts had to have been adaptive, *i.e.*, they had to have facilitated the organisms' reproduction or survival.

The survival value of cognitive capabilities is pretty obvious, but the very personal experience of encountering phenomena is not. So, then, why do we feel?

The question starts with,

> "[W]hat does this idea—the sensation with its phenomenal properties—'cause or enable or modify'? ...[I]f being conscious of feeling this way about the situation is to show up in behaviour, it must cause changes in your mental attitudes that dispose you to act in ways you wouldn't have done otherwise—the mental attitudes being the beliefs, hopes, and so on that you entertain about the situation or about yourself."

Id., p.89.

USEFULNESS?

The experience of a "feeling" likely encouraged a sense of an individualized "self." Increases in the range of such feelings may have stimulated a growing sense of self and prompted the emergence of self awareness and ultimately a type of consciousness. "[T]he level at which phenomenal quality does become relevant is not so much in your beliefs about the stimuli affecting you as in your beliefs about your self: that you are the being having the experience." *Id.*, p.106. "The upshot is that sensations come to be experienced as being inalienably private, suffused with distinctive modality-specific qualities, rooted in the thick time of the subjective present, **made of immaterial mind stuff**: in short, phenomenal." *Id.*, p.110 (emphasis added).

Humphrey believes that cognitive consciousness, *i.e.*, reasoning and intelligence, came before sentience. And, self awareness? That he does not directly address.

The main adaptive benefits of sentience, he asserts, come from the recognition that other beings are feeling creatures too and with feelings like one's own. The ability to examine one's own inner feelings and experiences enables an understanding of what others are thinking and the prediction of what they are likely to do.

> "When you see another individual—a mate, a mother, a friend, an enemy—as having a self like yours, you'll have a head start in understanding them and predicting their behaviour. I believe the importance of mind-reading in both directions may help explain features of phenomenal consciousness that would otherwise seem superfluous."
>
> ...
>
> "In the course of relatively recent history, those of our ancestors who thought of themselves as beings imbued with immaterial qualities, existing outside normal space and time,

will have taken their own existence ever more seriously. The more mysterious and unworldly the qualities of phenomenal consciousness, the more significant the self."

Id., pp.119, 118.

How might sentience have emerged?

POSSIBLE SOURCES

Humphrey theorizes that the first step was the appearance of the instinctive reflexive physical response to external stimuli. Then,

> "[A]s these animals evolve and begin to lead more complex lives, the time comes when reflex behaviour is not enough. If they are to behave more flexibly, they need to be able to store information about themselves and their environs in a form they can refer to offline. In particular, they need a way of representing and holding 'in mind' information about events occurring at their body surface."

Id., p.106.

At some point, an animal captures an internal image or representation of the reaction to the stimulus and experienced some sensation or feeling associated with it.

"An animal whose sensations lack a phenomenal dimension can still be cognitively conscious: that's to say it can have introspective access to

---

its mental states—perceptions, beliefs, desires, and so on—and show the intelligence that goes with this." *Id.*, p.147.

Humphrey explains that many researchers assume that "if we are to arrive at a transparent theory, we must discover the neural correlates of consciousness," but "[w]hen you see red, there won't be any activity of the brain that is phenomenally red; there will only be some activity by the brain that creates the idea of phenomenal redness." *Id.*, p.88. Thus, it is not "the neural correlates of consciousness but **the neural correlates of representing consciousness**" we need. *Id.*, p.86. "This means, in turn, that we should be looking for a two-stage process. First, there will be the brain activity that is the vehicle for the representation. Then, quite separately, there will the brain activity that takes this vehicle to point to the idea." *Id.*, p.88. "Your brain creates a representation of stimuli arriving at your sense organs, and you, the representee, read this in order to arrive at the idea of what the stimulation feels like." *Id.*, p.89.

"The outgoing commands, rather than causing an actual bodily response to the stimulus where it's occurring, begin to target the internal body map where the sense organs first project to the brain. ...Once motor signals that were formerly sent out to produce a response at a particular locus on the body surface have been redirected to the place in the brain where sensory signals from this locus come in, there's the potential for feedback."

...

"When conditions are ripe, the outgoing motor signals will be able to interact with the incoming sensory signals to create a self-entangling loop—a loop that can sustain recursive activity, flowing round and round, catching its own tail."

Id., p.109.

"Indeed, from here on, whenever the opportunity arises to 'improve' the quality of sensations, natural selection has a whole new design space to explore. Small tweaks to the circuitry can have dramatic effects on the subject's reading of what sensations feel like." *Id.*, p.110.

Humphrey speculates that the stimulus to the development of the capability to become sentient was the evolution of warm-bloodedness.

"I propose that warm-bloodedness played a double role in the evolution of sentience: on the one hand, it brought about changes in lifestyle that made sentience an essential psychological asset; on the other hand, it prepared the brain to deliver it. Being warm-blooded is expensive. Maintaining a constant high temperature requires a big expenditure of energy. ...[A]s temperature goes up various bodily processes actually become more energetically efficient, so the costs can be partially offset. A separate advantage is that warm-bloodedness provides a defence against infections by fungi and bacteria."

Id., p.149.

The result?

"[T]he more obvious one [is] that it allowed animals to ride out climatic changes and expand their geographic range. In body and in mind, they were becoming increasingly autonomous agents, with the freedom to go where they would when they would." *Id.*, p.150.

> That speculation is consistent with his conclusion that the only sentient animals are mammals and birds. "[Sentient animals] will be highly intelligent, especially in the social sphere, and have a strong sense of their own individual selfhood: for example, dogs, chimpanzees, parrots, humans. And who else? I'm going to narrow it down. I'm ready to argue that sentience is restricted to mammals and birds." *Id.*, p.147.

Humphrey sets forth several fascinating examples of humans and animals illustrating the nature of sentience and sensory perception.

Interestingly, both Humphrey and Sean Carroll, in the book discussed in the prior chapter, use a hypothetical proposed by Australian philosopher Frank Jackson in the 1980s, reaching different, but similar, conclusions.

Mary is a neuroscientist who knows everything there is to know about the color red, but she has never seen anything red. One day, Mary sees red.

Does she learn anything new?

Carroll says yes, obviously, but ...

"When she walks outside her room and those neurons do finally fire, does Mary 'learn something new'? In one sense, surely yes—she now has memories that she hadn't previously possessed. Knowledge is related to our capacity to answer questions and do things, and Mary can now do something she couldn't before: recognize red things by sight. Is this an argument that there is more to the universe than its physical aspects? Surely not. We have merely introduced an artificial distinction between two kinds of collections of synaptic connections: 'ones induced by reading literature and doing scientific experiments in black and white,' and 'ones induced by stimulating the visual cortex by seeing red photons.' ...It's a difference in the way the knowledge got to your brain, not in the kind of knowledge it is."

Sean M. Carroll, *The Big Picture: On the Origins of Life, Meaning, and the Universe Itself* (2016), p.353.

Humphrey says not really, but...

"[W]e should expect Mary to be ahead of the game. As an expert psychologist, she will have seen it all at the level of behaviour; as a neuroscientist, she'll have seen it at the level of brain activity. So, she'll know everything you yourself know and more. ...It follows that when Mary first sees red she will be epistemically totally prepared. She will not gain any new knowledge from the new experience. This isn't to say it won't be a new experience for her. Of course it will."

...

'Nonetheless, **the attitudes about seeing red she finds herself having as a consequence of her experience will be exactly those she would have predicted**. ...[I]f there are essential features of phenomenal consciousness that could not in principle be discovered through outside scientific observation, we would be hard put to explain how these features could have evolved. If a scientist like Mary couldn't know about a particular feature, nor could natural selection."

Sentience, pp.96-8 (emphasis added).

Both are quick to defend their respective hypotheses, but I find both responses a bit facile. Carroll asserts that the only difference is how the information was received by Mary. That, of course, depends on the definition of "knowledge." Book learning and the experience of red are certainly different and involve different parts of the brain. But, I do not think his response (or the hypothetical) really addresses the question posed by determinism. The hypothetical challenges physicalism, suggesting that there are things existing that have no physical components.

Humphrey also seems to overreact. He is concerned that the hypothetical suggests that natural selection could not have operated on sentience if the phenomena are not susceptible to scientists. Like the common confusion between genes and traits, which I discussed in *Important Things*, Humphrey momentarily forgets that natural selection deals with the consequences of the mutation, not the mutation itself.

We should just admit that Mary had a new experience and learned something. The question to address is what are the implications?

SO…

It seems that, "consciousness transforms how your mind works on two levels: (a) it creates a cognitive workspace, which makes you more intelligent; (b) it underwrites a coherent selfnarrative, which helps you make sense of your own and others' behaviour." *Id.,* p.6.

Jeremy Bentham, quoted at the beginning, advocated for animal rights on the grounds that certain animals feel pain. Those that do are special. But, still, "[t]he chasm is awesome."

> "The emotional lives of men and of other mammals are indeed marvelously similar. But to focus upon the similarity unduly is to forget that such a chasm exists at all. The intellectual life of man, his culture and history and religion and science, is different from anything else we know of in the universe."

Julian Jaynes, *The Origin of Consciousness in the Breakdown of the Bicameral Mind* (1976) (2000 edition), p.9.

So, there still is the matter of introspection and self-awareness—the "much more" than what may be found in other animals. A whole different level. Perhaps, the notion of a feedback loop is a clue. It seems quite possible that emerging sentience played a role. Obviously, the adaptive benefits are strong: enhanced social and political skills, planning for the future, a variety of new mental states and the evolution of empathy. These capabilities would indeed appear necessary for community living, urbanization and much of what we call civilization, including the arts, literature and the sciences.

Relativity and Origins

CHAPTER 17

Matter and Energy

Pythagoras to Einstein
via
Newton, Maxwell and Lorentz

I.

1. Pythagoras was born in Samos (Greece) and lived for about 70 years during the sixth century BCE. A famous theorem is named for him. Historians tell us, however, that he was not the first to discover the relationship we now call the Pythagorean Theorem (there is evidence of knowledge of the relationship in Babylon dating to some 1000 years earlier and in India dating to a few hundreds of years earlier). In fact, he may not have even been aware of it (it was credited to him by his followers only several generations-—some 150 years—after his death).

2. The Theorem has played an important role in the development of scientific understanding. It states that the length of the hypotenuse of a right triangle (the longest side which is opposite the 90 degree "right" angle) is equal to the square root of the sum of the squares of the other two sides. If the two shorter sides are A and B and the hypotenuse

is C, then $A^2+B^2=C^2$. If one travels east A miles, then north B miles, our new location will be how far "as the crow flies" from the starting point? You will have traveled A+B miles, and our intuition tells that our distance from the starting point will be less than A+B but greater than either A or B. The Pythagorean Theorem says that the distance, "as the crow flies," will be the square root of A^2+B^2, which clearly falls between A+B and A or B. Indeed, if one then were able to go straight up for E miles, this new position would be from our original starting point, as the crow flies, the distance of the square root of C', where C' is the hypotenuse of a new right triangle with one side equal to C and one to E (the amount of the elevation with the right angle at the point of liftoff).

3. Why are the answers based on squares? The reason arises from the fact that the area of a square is equal to the square of any of its sides. The Theorem tells us that the area of A^2 plus the area of B^2 will be equal to the area of C^2. I have read that there are more than 300 proofs of the Pythagorean Theorem that have been presented over the years. Here is one:

> Take a square with sides equal to C, so with an area of C^2. Place four of our right triangles around the square with the hypotenuse of each (length C) on each of the sides of the square. The result is a bigger square with sides of the length A+B and, so, an area of $(A+B)^2$, which equals $A^2+2AB+B^2$. Each right triangle has an area of 1/2AB (half of a rectangle AB), and there are four of them, plus the area C^2, within the area of $(A+B)^2$. So, the area of the smaller square C^2 must equal the area of the large square $(A+B)^2$, minus the sum of the areas of the four triangles. Or, $C^2=A^2+2AB+B^2$ minus 2AB, which is A^2+B^2.

There are numerous variations of this proof based on a square of sides C and four of the right triangles ABC.

4. Now, back to my example above. If we add to the various sides of the triangles the direction we traveled on each leg of our journey, we can call them "vectors" (each with a direction and a distance, given by the position and the length). We can see that C' represents the "sum" of the other two vectors added together end-to-end (using C only once). And, they can be added in any order as long as we start from the same place. Visualize the vectors placed on a graph. Both the x-axis and the y-axis will be in units of distance (feet, kilometers, *etc.*). The distance traveled east will be the change in position along the x-axis (Δx) and the distance traveled north will be Δy. Thus, the hypotenuse will be the square root of $\Delta x^2 + \Delta y^2$.

5. Suppose we want to depict a vector in spacetime (in four dimensions)? Then, one of the axes will be time, while the other will be distance, *i.e.*, the final vector determined in three dimensional space (a sum of vectors). But, how do we generate a vector when the two axes are in different types of measures? One solution is to multiply the "time" axis by a particular velocity d/t (*e.g.*, kilometers per second). But, what do we use for velocity? As we learned from Einstein's special theory, in spacetime, time and distance are not invariable—they depend upon the observer. One thing that is invariable in the Special Theory is the speed of light or, more accurately, the speed of a particle with no mass. The universal speed limit. Customarily, we refer to that speed as "c." Thus, one axis (usually the vertical) is ct, and the other one is d. The length of the vector is the square root of $\Delta ct^2 + \Delta d^2$. We can label the length of the vector "s."

6. Then $s^2 = \Delta ct^2 + \Delta d^2$, assuming spacetime is "flat" (in the Euclidean sense). If it is "Minkowski spacetime," then $s^2 = \Delta ct^2 - \Delta d^2$ (*i.e.*, minus rather than plus). And, spacetime must be hyperbolic to comport with our sense of causation.

"If we decide to define the distance in spacetime between the two events O and A using Pythagoras' equation but with a minus sign, then no matter how anyone views the two events, A never crosses into O's past; it just moves around on the hyperbola. This means that if event A is in O's future according to one observer, then every other observer will also agree that A is in O's future too."

Brian Cox and Jeff Forshaw, *Why Does E=mc²? (And Why Should We Care?)* (2009), p. 84.

$\Delta s/c$ is a measure of time (distance divided by speed). And, Δs divided by $\Delta s/c$ (distance divided by time) equals c.

7. Momentum is defined as mass times velocity, p=mv. Momentum can be described by vectors; only the axes are different. (All momentum vectors in spacetime will have a length of "mc.") Velocity is distance/time (and acceleration is the change in velocity). Thus, momentum p is mass (m) times $\Delta d/\Delta t$: $p=m\Delta d/\Delta t$. And, we can write the equation replacing Δd with Δs and Δt with $\Delta s/c$ to get $p=m \Delta s/\Delta s/c$. But, $\Delta s/c$ is equal to the square root of $(\Delta ct^2-\Delta d^2)/c$ (in hyperbolic space). So, $p=m\Delta s/$square root of $(\Delta ct^2-\Delta d^2)/c$.

II.

$E=mc^2$

1. The traditional proofs of $E=mc^2$ begin with the Special Theory of Relativity. Remember Einstein's example of the light clock? We have two mirrors, one is stationary and the other is moving, relative to the first, at a constant speed "v". The mirrors are a distance apart of "d" when a light just above the stationary mirror flashes. If both mirrors were stationary, the return flash would be received 2d/c seconds later,

since the light has traveled there and back, a distance of 2d, at the speed of light c, and the time taken is distance/speed. We will label this time as "t". But, since the second mirror is moving at speed v, the light will actually travel the hypotenuse of a right triangle with sides of d and time T (the longer time from the greater distance traveled) multiplied by v. We know that the distance is equal to cT. According to the Theorem, the distance actually traveled between the mirrors is also the square root of $d^2+(vT)^2$. (The round trip will be twice that.) We can state that $cT=\sqrt{(d^2+(vT)^2)}$. We can then treat d as being equal 1, giving $cT=\sqrt{((1^2-vT)^2)}$ where $t=1/c$ and $c=1/t$. Replacing c with $1/t$ and dividing by T, we get $1/t=\sqrt{((1^2-(vT)^2)/T}$ and $t=1/\sqrt{((1^2-(vT)^2)/T}$. To an observer located with the moving mirror, however, only time t (2d/c) will have past, so the difference between time experienced by the two observers reflects the impact of the velocity on the passage of time for the moving observer.

"[I]t is running slow by a factor of $c/\sqrt{c^2 - v^2}$."

Cox and Forshaw, *Why Does E=mc2?*, p. 48.

We can also use t and d/c as coordinates in units of time (distance/speed equals time). Then the length of the hypotenuse will represent the amount of time that has passed in that frame of reference. If the person is standing still, $\Delta(d/c)$ is zero and, so, the time passed is t (*i.e.*, $\sqrt{(t^2)}$. If we substitute for $\Delta(d/c)$ the expression $v\Delta t$ (*i.e.*, velocity times the change in time), then we get the square of the time in timespace is equal to $\Delta t^2-v^2\Delta t^2$ or $(1-v^2)(\Delta t)^2$. And, the time elapsed in timespace is $\sqrt{(1-v^2\Delta t^2)}$.

See Sean M. Carroll, *The Biggest Ideas in the Universe: Space, Time, and Motion* (2023), pp.151-5.

So, the amount by which our momentum vector moves in the time direction (the vertical side of the right triangle) is cΔt times m, divided by $1+1/2(v^2/c^2)$. If we multiply by the constant c, we get $mc^2+1/2mv^2$. The $1/2mv^2$ is kinetic energy (energy from movement).

And the "mc^2"? Let's call that "energy" or E.

We have: $E=mc^2$.

2. In 1904, Hendrik Lorentz (July 18, 1853—Feb. 4, 1928) derived what we now call the Lorentz Transformations, which describe the the shortening of the length of an object in motion relative to another object, as well as the dilation of time, reflecing the relationships between the relative velocity and both time and distance. The operative element ("the Lorentz Factor") is the expression:

$$1/ \sqrt{1} - v^2/c^2$$

Physicists claim that this expression can be derived mathematically from the equations we generated in the paragraphs above. (I take their word for it.)

III.

1. Curiously, the relativity of time and of distance are not directly connected to energy or mass. The key proposition is the relationship between mass and velocity, *i.e.*, mass increases when the speed of an object increases. That transformation does not depend on Special Relativity; it arises out of Maxwell's field equations for electromagnetic waves.

2.. In his textbook *Lectures on Physics*, Richard Feynman begins the chapter on Special Relativity (Volume 1, Chapter 15) as follows:

"For over 200 years the equations of motion enunciated by Newton were believed to describe nature correctly, and the first time that an error in these laws was discovered, the way to correct it was also discovered. Both the error and its correction were discovered by Einstein in 1905.

"Newton's Second Law, which we have expressed by the equation $F=d(mv)/dt$ was stated with the tacit assumption that m is a constant, but we now know that this is not true, and that the mass of a body increases with velocity. In Einstein's corrected formula m has the value $m'=m/\sqrt{1-v^2/c^2}$ where the rest mass represents the mass of a body that is not moving and c is the speed of light... .

"For those who want to learn just enough about it so they can solve problems, that is all there is to the theory of relativity—it just changes Newton's laws by introducing a correction factor to the mass."

Similarly,

"As a result of the entire study, the following conclusions can be drawn:

- The equivalence energy-mass is not necessarily a relativistic principle but, as Einstein himself proved ..., a principle derivable from the laws of classical physics.
- The constancy of the speed of light in vacuum, which is valid for all inertial systems, is not a postulate to be assumed *a priori*, but a principle provable by the laws of physics.
- If Newtonian mechanics, with reference to the second law of motion, is pursued as the leading approach, then the theory of relativity can be regarded as a consequence of the equivalence principle of energy-mass."

Cester, Clemente, Korff, *Newton and Relativity,* Introduction.

3. Or, consider the following:

"Maxwell's electromagnetic equations have demonstrated that light travels at a constant speed ... [and] the momentum (p) of electromagnetic waves, or photons, is proportional to their energy level (E):

$$(1) \quad p=E/c$$
$$\text{or}$$
$$(2) \quad E=pc$$

"In Newtonian physics, the momentum (p) of an object is defined as

$$(3) \quad p=mv$$

where m is the mass of the object, and v is the velocity. In the case of a photon, the definition can be simplified below since a photon travels at the speed of light (c),

$$(4) \quad p=mc$$

"Now, replace p in equation (2) with the momentum given in equation (4), and we found the mass-energy equation:

$$(5) \quad E=mc^2.$$

"So simple, isn't it?

"Wait a second, a photon does not have mass. ...When people say a photon has no mass, they are referring to the rest/invariant mass, which is typically denoted by m_0. The mass in the ...

equations refers to the relativistic mass. In the case of a photon, there is no rest mass, but it still possesses relativistic mass. For a stationary object, its relativistic mass has the same value as its rest mass."

Jerry Z. Liu, "The Simplest Derivation of E=mc²," Stanford University (1998).

4. Relativist mass? The assertion is that mass is affected by motion. The resting or inertial mass will be less than the mass of an object in motion, increasing as the velocity approaches the speed of light. But, what if the object has no inertial mass, like a photon? A photon at rest? What does that even mean? Light (photons) is seen to travel in a vacuum at "the speed of light" by all observers. So, what is the relativist mass of a photon traveling at speed c? For particles with inertial mass, the relativist mass increases exponentially as its speed approaches c. That is one reason that such a particle cannot ever travel at or above the speed of light—its mass would become infinite. So, what is the mass of particles that do travel at the speed of light? Here is the formula for relativistic mass (m'):

$$m'=m/\sqrt{1 - v^2/c^2}$$

But, if resting m is zero, then we have a fraction with a numerator of zero, which must equal zero. If velocity reaches c, we get a fraction with a denominator of zero, which has a value that is undefined.

IV.

1. James Clerk Maxwell (June 13, 1831-November 5, 1879) concluded that light and other electromagnetic waves exert a force on objects that they strike. It is called "radiation pressure." It has been experimentally observed.

2. A theoretical proof that $E=mc^2$ has been proposed as follows. If objects A and B are at rest relative to one another and A emits a flash of light towards B, A will be pushed further from A by the recoil. However, the center of gravity of AB would not change. So, we conclude that the mass of B must have increased and the mass of A decreased.

> "From this it can be concluded that because of the emission of the light beam, the body K1 on the left, which is located at the greater distance from the center of gravity, must have decreased by a certain mass Δ� that has yet to be calculated. On the other hand, since the total mass of the system remains unchanged, the mass of the body K2 on the right must necessarily have increased by the same amount Δ�.

> "It follows that after the absorption of the light beam the mass of the body K2 has become m + Δm and the mass of the body K1 has become m−Δm.

> "It can therefore be concluded that:

> - The emission of a light beam with the energy E by a body causes a decrease of the mass of the body itself, which is equal to the energy of the light beam divided by the square of the speed of light.
> - The absorption of a light beam with the energy E by a body causes an increase in the mass of the body itself, equal to the energy of the light beam divided by the square of the speed of light."

Cester, Clemente, Korff, *Newton and Relativity*, Chapter 3.

The assertion that the object emitting the flash of light experiences "recoil" assumes the existence of "radiation pressure," rather than proving it. The recoil is a matter of fact. If it is observed, then the theory sets out a possible explanation of how, and perhaps why, it occurs.

3. Gravitational waves contain energy. Interestingly, when an asymmetry in two colliding black holes cause the gravitational waves to be emitted in one direction, the force of the waves is such as to push the black hole in the other direction. "If the pair's convergence blows gravitational waves preferentially in one direction, then the emerging black hole will recoil in the opposite direction at high speed, like kickback from a gun." Nikk Ogasa, "Recoiling black holes could move at nearly one-tenth the speed of light: The cosmic sinkholes gain speed from being kicked by gravitational waves," *ScienceNews,* August 18, 2023.

V.

Laws of Conservation

1. I have not discussed the "laws of conservation," conservation of mass, of energy, of momentum, and so on. Although physicists offer proofs of these laws, here I simply treat these laws as necessary assumptions or axioms of the theories of mechanics. "Although these conservation laws were originally formulated within a Newtonian worldview, their very general nature suggested to Einstein that they might have a wider validity. Therefore, as a working hypothesis, he assumed them to be satisfied *in all inertial frames*, and explored the consequences." Nikk Ogasa, "Recoiling black holes could move at nearly one-tenth the speed of light: The cosmic sinkholes gain speed from being kicked by gravitational waves," *ScienceNews,* August 18, 2023.

2. Once we introduce the relativity of time, the results of the collision of two bodies (say, spaceships or planets) traveling at different speeds

will not reflect the conservation of momentum from the perspective of observers on both objects. Or, if radiation pressure exists, then the law of conservation of momentum would require that the massless particle traveling at the speed of light has momentum. Since, momentum equals mass times velocity, the particle with momentum must have mass.

3.

> "Einstein was so sure that momentum conservation must always hold that he rescued it with a bold hypothesis: the mass of an object must depend on its speed! In fact, the mass must increase with speed in just such a way as to cancel out the smaller ... velocity resulting from time dilation.
>
> ...
>
> "Deciding that masses of objects must depend on speed like this seems a heavy price to pay to rescue conservation of momentum!"

Michael Fowler, University of Virginia, *Modern Physics.*

(As we have seen, it is a common and accepted scientific practice to assume something is true, or not true, and derive the consequences.)

4. Yet,

> "[I]t is a prediction that is not difficult to check by experiment. The first confirmation came in 1908, measuring the mass of fast electrons in a vacuum tube.
>
> ...

"[I]n modern particle accelerators very powerful electric fields are used to accelerate electrons, protons and other particles. It is found in practice that these particles become heavier and heavier as the speed of light is approached, and hence need greater and greater forces for further acceleration. Consequently, the speed of light is a natural absolute speed limit."

...

"We have therefore established that transfer of energy implies transfer of the equivalent mass."

Id.

VI.

1. What is the physics explanation for the relationship between mass and speed?

"[H]ow is this mass transfer physically realized? Is the front end of the tube really heavier after it absorbs the light? The answer is yes, because it's a bit hotter, which means its atoms are vibrating slightly faster and faster moving objects have higher mass (or, if you prefer, higher mass-energy)."

Id.

2. The empirical evidence seems to be consistent with the conclusion that photons (light) have relativist mass. And, virtually everything we identify as not traveling at the speed of light is moving at only a very small percentage of that speed, so the impact of velocity on mass is typically infinitesimal. Back to vectors. A particle traveling at the speed of light will exhaust its movement in spacetime through its movement

through space. It will have no movement through time. Thus, it will be timeless. A particle that is motionless in space (based upon the coordinates selected—its frame of reference) will have all of its movement through spacetime in movement through time.

3. Let's go back to that minus sign. We have concluded that everything must move through spacetime at the speed c. That means that there is a necessary trade off between time and space—the greater the distance traveled through time, the less the distance traveled through space. Thus, the relationship between time squared and distance squared in Pythagoras' Theorem must be one of subtraction, not an addiction. We have not proven anything. We have simply identified what our assumption might mean. The "proof" is in terms of the "cone of light" and our experience of past and future.

4. Is this "relativist mass" actually "mass"? Well, we have not really defined mass. "Mass ... is an intrinsic property; roughly speaking, mass is the resistance that an object has to being accelerated." Sean M. Carroll, *The Biggest Ideas in the Universe: Space, Time, and Motion* (2023), p.12. Mass, whatever it is, displays inertia (and momentum) and is subject to gravity. "[T]he 'relativistic mass' indeed has the two basic properties of mass: inertia and gravitational attraction. (...[T]his relativistic mass is nothing but the total energy, with the rest mass itself now seen as 'rest energy'.) ...So we see that in the general case the work done on the body, by definition its kinetic energy, is just equal to its mass increase multiplied by c^2." Michael Fowler, University of Virginia, *Modern Physics*.

5. Thus, we conclude that $E=mc^2$ simply asserts the equivalence of mass and energy. If the energy of an object changes, then the mass of the object will also change in the same direction and in an amount given by the formula $\Delta m=\Delta E/c^2$. The formula itself says nothing about whether or how mass can be converted to energy or *vice versa*. But, it does provide the "exchange rate" if a conversion were to occur.

6. And, we find that massless particles moving at the speed of light have "mass," because they have energy. As a result, such particles can convey a force and are subject to gravity. But, it is a little misleading to call them "particles." Yet, what is a particle with a resting mass anyway? Just something that reacts to the Higg's Boson? Does a particle with no resting mass interact with a Higg's Boson when moving at the speed of light? If not, then does it really have mass? ("Early thinkers, including Newton himself, didn't quite appreciate that momentum and energy were two separate things; they thought in terms of a single 'quantity of motion.'" Carroll, p.22.)

"Weirdly, however, things that are definitely not matter, can contribute to something's mass... .When it comes to protons and neutrons, only a fraction of their mass comes from their matter components (the quarks). The rest comes from various kinds of energy involved in holding the quarks together."

Katie Mack, "Many questions remain unanswered when it comes to matter, but the biggest one is: Why is there any matter to begin with?" *BBC Science Focus,* New Year Issue, December 2023.

"Under relativity, energy and momentum are both conserved..., but mass is just a particular kind of energy." Carroll, p.23.

VII.

Matter and Energy

1. So, for that matter, what is energy?

"Energy isn't a kind of substance, like water or dirt. It's a property that things have, depending on what they are and what kind of situation they're in. There is no 'energy fluid' that flows from place to place. There are simply objects that have positions and velocities and other properties, and we can associate a certain amount of energy with them because of those facts."

Carroll, p.8.

(And, mass also is "an intrinsic property" that "isn't a kind of substance, like water or dirt. It's a property that things have, depending on what they are and what kind of situation they're in.")

"...Einstein's theory recognises that the source of gravity is not mass, as Newton believed, but energy, one form of which is mass. This means that all forms of energy have gravity: sound energy, heat energy and so on. ... Crucially, gravity itself is a form of energy, so gravity creates more gravity."

Marcus Chown, "Newton vs Einstein: what is the major discrepancy between their theories of gravity?" *BBC Sky at Night Magazine*, 19 January 2024 (originally appeared in the December 2006).

---

2. A more traditional definition is the capacity to perform work. Potential energy derives from an object's position, like a ball at the top of a hill. Release it and as it starts to roll down hill, the potential energy is converted to kinetic energy, energy arising from motion and reflected in the object's momentum. Now, in fact, the potential energy is a result of gravity. A ball in outer space, free from gravitational forces, will have no potential energy regardless of its position. Release it and it does not move. An object's kinetic energy, like its motion, is the result of the application of some force, gravity or something propelling it (like a push). Besides gravity, sources of propulsion include chemical and nuclear reactions. "Energy" contained in the atoms or in the nuclei is released as matter is converted to energy. Physicists talk about the conservation of energy, theorizing that the total amount in the Universe remains the same, only the forms change.

3. How does energy flow with an electric current? We talk about electrons moving through a conductor, but no one electron moves very far. In a DC circuit, the electrons displace some of their neighbors, who in turn displace their neighbors and so on down the wire. In an AC circuit, the electrons very rapidly move forward then backwards as the current alternates direction. Do the electrons carry energy and pass it on? Apparently not. The movements of the electrons create electro-magnetic fields around the conductor, perpendicular to it (radiating outward, encircling the wire). The energy flow is through those electro-magnetic fields. They carry or transmit the energy. The energy flow continues in one direction even with alternating current because the fields flip back and forth.

"Intuition would seem to tell us that the electrons get their energy from being pushed along the wire, so the energy should be flowing down (or up) along the wire. But the theory says that the electrons are really being pushed

---

---

by an electric field, which has come from some charges very far away, and that the electrons get their energy for generating heat from these fields."

Feynman Lectures on Physics, Vol. II, Chapter 27, "Field Energy and Field Momentum" (27–5 Examples of energy flow).

---

4. Okay. But, what again is energy?

VIII.

1. We have been discussing mass, but what about "matter"? The equation $E=mc^2$ is said to contemplate the transformation of matter into energy, like with the atomic bomb. Mass is the characteristic of matter that corresponds to the amount of energy that can be produced by the conversion. But, what is matter? We know that it is something that has inertia and is subject to gravity. We assume that it consists of particles in some combination.

2. What about "dark matter" and "antimatter"? Dark matter is subject to gravity. That is how we know it exists. But, that is about all we know about it. Antimatter is theorized to have existed at the beginning of the Universe. It is supposedly identical to normal matter except the opposite, so the encounter between a particle and its opposite results in the annihilation of both. Recent experiments have confirmed that antimatter is subject to gravity, when dropped, it falls toward the Earth.

"[T]he ALPHA-g experiment showed that antimatter does, in fact, fall down. As far as gravity is concerned, antimatter is, really, just matter. Back in September, researchers at CERN managed to create and capture a sample of antihydrogen (the antimatter version of hydrogen). They held the sample in a magnetic field so precarious that any slight misalignment would cause it to annihilate against the walls of its container. And then they dropped it."

Katie Mack, December 2023.

So, all types of matter have mass. But, that does not really answer the question, because energy, and even gravity itself, has mass.

IX.

This chapter has concerned "classical" theories of physics. Today's Standard Model of particle physics is a quantum field (non-classical). That describes matter quite differently.

"In quantum field theories, the basic building blocks of the universe are fields, not particles. There is a field for each of the particles in nature.... . In a quantum field, ripples can occur only in certain discrete sizes. The smallest possible ripple in a given field is what we call a particle; positive ripples in the field are matter particles, and negative ripples in the field are antimatter particles. ...The amount of energy it takes to create the smallest possible ripple depends on the stiffness of the [field]; this minimum amount of energy is the rest mass of the associated particle. The different fields are linked together—or 'coupled'—so that a ripple in one field disturbs the connected fields.an electron—a ripple in the electron field—disturbs the electromagnetic field around it. ...What we call an electron is actually a composite excitation of all these fields, like a large water wave causing disturbances in the air above it."

Luke Caldwell, "The Mystery of Matter," *Scientific American Magazine*, February 2024, p. 52.

"In modern physics, fields are the fundamental building blocks of reality (to the best of our current knowledge). ...At any point in space, each field is being pushed around by other fields, but only by the values (and derivatives) of other fields at precisely the same point in space."

Sean M. Carroll, *The Biggest Ideas in the Universe: Space, Time, and Motion* (2023), p.113.

SO?

Now, all of this may seem like only a bunch of definitions connected by logical (mathematical) statements. Like in numerous other situations in science that we have discussed, one cannot help but wonder whether we have generated anything more than logical circles. The important caveat, however, is that this "theory" enables predictions of great accuracy (and, therefore, of great utility). But, does the theory therefore represent reality?

No.

CHAPTER 18

Origins

New, improved tools continue to supply us with new data concerning the Universe, which we then assess in light of our current theories. If the data is consistent with the theories, scientists will note the apparent confirmation. If the new data is not, we start imagining again. I briefly describe some recent examples.

THE "JWST" AND THE AGE OF THE UNIVERSE

The James Webb Space Telescope ("JWST"), operational since January 2021, has certainly met expectations. The photographs resulting, regularly posted by NASA, are amazing, often beyond belief. Among the many discoveries of the JWST is the identification of what may be the oldest galaxy and the oldest star in the Universe.

For example:

"Using the JWST's Near Infrared Spectrograph, the study authors parsed the light of two ancient objects: Maisie's galaxy and CEERS-93316, another galaxy that was discovered around the same time and was initially estimated to exist just 250 million years after the Big Bang. ...While the team's spectroscopic analysis confirmed that Maisie's galaxy is indeed as distant and ancient as its brightness suggests, the same was not true for CEERS-93316. After splitting the galaxy's light, the researchers found that globs of hot hydrogen and oxygen contained there were emitting light so intensely that they made the whole galaxy appear bluer — and hence older — than it actually was... ."

Brandon Specktor, "13 billion-year-old 'Maisie's galaxy' is one of the oldest objects in the universe, James Webb telescope reveals," *Live Science,* August 17, 2023.

And:

"Astronomers have used the James Webb Space Telescope to observe Earendel, the most distant star ever detected. ...Earendel is so distant that the starlight glimpsed by the Webb telescope was emitted within the first billion years of the universe. The universe is estimated to be about 13.8 billion years old. ...Previous estimates suggest the star is 12.9 billion light-years away from Earth, but given the expansion of the universe and how long the light has traveled to reach us, astronomers believe Earendel is currently 28 billion light-years away."

Ashley Strickland, "Webb telescope captures image of most distant star ever seen," *CNN,* August 11, 2023.

The complication is that these objects appear to be too old, to have appeared too close in time to the beginning of the Universe (the Big Bang).

> "These galaxies, existing a mere 300 million years or so after the Big Bang, appear to have a level of maturity and mass typically associated with billions of years of cosmic evolution. Furthermore, they're surprisingly small in size, adding another layer of mystery to the equation."

Bernard Rizk, "New research puts age of universe at 26.7 billion years, nearly twice as old as previously believed," *phys.org*, July 13, 2023.

The current cosmological theories assume that the Universe consisted of extremely hot plasma for the first 300,000 years, only then did matter begin to form. It should have taken many hundreds of millions of additional years for the emergence of stars and then galaxies.

> "[T]he standard model of cosmology... predicts that, as we look farther and farther back in time—*i.e.*, to greater and greater cosmic distances—that the galaxies we see will be inherently smaller, bluer, less evolved, less rich in heavy elements, and that at some point beyond where we've been able to look, we should cease to see stars or galaxies of any type. ...Many of these early galaxies that JWST is finding have peculiar, puzzling properties about them that appear difficult to reconcile with this theoretical picture that the Universe has painted for us."

Ethan Siegel, "Ask Ethan: Do JWST's results contradict the Big Bang? JWST has brought us more distant views of the early Universe than ever before. Is the Big Bang, and all of modern cosmology, in trouble?," *Starts With A Bang*, April 21, 2023.

So, should we question the interpretations of the data from the JWST or the existing cosmological theories? We look to (and for) empirical verification of our scientific theories, and supposedly reject disconfirmed theories.

As previously discussed, our understanding of the age and expansion of the Universe derives from the analysis of the redshift phenomenon or Doppler Effect. Separately, most cosmologists now accept the inflation theory, which postulates something rather different from what gives rise to the Doppler Effect: "a combination of the Doppler shift due to relative velocity, gravitational redshift due to the curvature of spacetime, and cosmological redshift due to the expansion of the Universe." Ethan Siegel, "Is the Universe 13.8 or 26.7 billion years old? *Big Think: Starts with a Bang*, July 18, 2023.

Rajendra Gupta from the University of Ottawa has announced a model that calculates the age of the Universe as roughly twice as long as the current consensus. R Gupta, "JWST early Universe observations and ΛCDM cosmology," *Royal Astronomical Society*, 07 July 2023.

> "Impossible early galaxies refer to the fact that some galaxies dating to the cosmic dawn — 500 to 800 million years after the big bang — have discs and bulges similar to those which have passed through a long period of evolution. And smaller in size galaxies are apparently more massive than larger ones, which is quite the opposite of expectation."

Rajendra Gupta, "How old is the universe exactly? A new theory suggests that it's been around for twice as long as believed," *The Conversation*, August 28, 2023.

A theory propounded by Fritz Zwicky in 1929 says that light gradually loses energy, gets tired, over long periods of time. Such a phenomenon would itself cause a redshift in the observed frequency of the light.

"Zwicky's tired light theory proposes that the redshift of light from distant galaxies is due to the gradual loss of energy by photons over vast cosmic distances. However, it was seen to conflict with observations. Gupta found that 'by allowing this theory to coexist with the expanding universe, it becomes possible to reinterpret the redshift as a hybrid phenomenon, rather than purely due to expansion.'"

Rizk, "New research puts age of universe at 26.7 billion years, nearly twice as old as previously believed," *phys.org*, July 13, 2023.

Gupta's model involves "a few subtle-but-important changes." Siegel, "Is the Universe 13.8 or 26.7 billion years old?"

"First, ...Gupta ... presupposes ... the tired-light hypothesis, or the notion that light, as it travels through space, inherently 'radiates' and loses energy as it travels, becoming 'tired' before it arrives at the observer."

"And second, ... Gupta invokes an assumption that others have explored previously: that the fundamental constants c (the speed of light), $\hbar$ (Planck's constant), and G (the gravitational constant) aren't actually constant in time, but vary. In particular, they vary in a special way — **changing all together — so that the combinations of these constants that govern atomic transitions and the emission/absorption lines that we wind up observing, won't change as we look to earlier, more distant galaxies within the expanding Universe.**"

Id. (emphasis added).

"Gupta contends that, whereas JWST has shown us galaxies that appear brighter, more massive, and more evolved than had been expected to be seen so early on, his modified cosmology, with tired light and varying coupling constants, these galaxies suddenly fall into line with expectations."

Segal, "Ask Ethan: Do JWST's results contradict the Big Bang?"

Yet,

"It's entirely possible, even if these early galaxies are as bright and massive as the most optimistic estimates are, that boring old gravitation, electromagnetism, and stellar/gas physics can explain what we see."

Id.

GRAVITATIONAL WAVES

Gravitational waves are predicted by the General Theory of Relativity. Some suggestive signs were found early in the late twentieth century, but the first experimental evidence was reported from a very sensitive instrument called LIGO (Laser Interferometer Gravitational-Wave Observatory) in 2015-6. These gravitational waves arose when two black holes crashed into one another. The collision happened 1.3 billion years ago, but the ripples reached Earth only in 2015.

"Gravitational waves, like electromagnetic radiation, come in a range of frequencies with high-frequency gravitational waves, like high-frequency light, having shorter wavelengths and being more energetic while low-frequency gravitational waves have longer wavelengths and are less energetic. Low-frequency longwave gravitational waves also have long periods, the time it takes between one peak of the wave passing a set point to the next peak passing that point."

Robert Lea, "The universe is humming with gravitational waves. Here's why scientists are so excited about the discovery," *Space.com,* July 03, 2023.

The "noise" existing on Earth severely limits the detection of gravitational waves except from close and massive events. Construction of a LIGO in outer space, like on the Moon, would solve the problem, but it is not easily done.

An alternative method of detecting the waves was developed and in July 2023 appears to have been successful, finding evidence of background waves far too old and too distant to register on LIGO.

"[N]eutron stars['] ... magnetic fields act to channel particles to the poles of pulsars, where they are blasted out as jets at near-lightspeed from each pole. Pulsars appear to blink 'on and off' ... at incredibly precise regular intervals. ... The compression and stretching of spacetime as gravitational waves wash through it should have a discernible on the timing of pulsars, either slowing them down or speeding them up as they pass. This causes a very slight difference in the arrival time of light from these pulsars. Because the effect is small, pulsar timing arrays need to consist of many widely dispersed pulsars that have to be monitored for years."

Robert Lea, "The universe is humming with gravitational waves. Here's why scientists are so excited about the discovery," *Space.com*, July 03, 2023.

"On Thursday, June 28, the North American Nanohertz Observatory for Gravitational Waves (NANOGrav) revealed the detection of low-frequency gravitational waves, a historic breakthrough that represents 15 years of searching."

Id.

"'We have solid evidence for a hum of gravitational waves in a new band of the gravitational wave spectrum. These frequencies are 10-12 orders of magnitude smaller than those detected by LIGO, and have wavelengths light years long... .'"

Will Dunham, "Scientists discover that universe is awash in gravitational," Reuters, June 29, 2023 (quoting Jeff Hazboun, lead author of one of the papers describing the findings).

Now what? Confirmation or food for further imaginings?

And, So?

CHAPTER 19

What I Believe

"...I would live my time believing in a grand thing
that ought to be true if it is not.
No facts can take the place of truths,
and if these be not truths,
then is the loftiest part of our nature a waste.
Let me hold by the better than the actual... ."

George McDonald
Thomas Wingfold, Curate

My physical surroundings began to shrink in 2015. Further and further. Smaller and smaller. No more transAtlantic flights. No more visits to France. No more travel. No walks, no stairs, no narrow doorways. But, my world continued to expand. Emotionally, spiritually, mentally. Slowly at first, but more rapidly beginning in 2018.

While my body continued to weaken, my consciousness asserted itself more and more forcefully.

As Emily Dickinson wrote:

> **"The Brain—is wider than the Sky—**
> **For—put them side by side—**
> **The one the other will contain**
> **With ease—and you—beside—."**

"The Brain Is Wider Than the Sky" (1863)

In 2018, as I was finishing a substantial revision (fourth edition) of my first book *Important Things* (the first edition in 2016 titled *Limits of Science?*), I had a revelation of sorts. I wanted to state it explicitly, so I wrote a postscript. And, in the Preface, I advised readers as follows:

"If you say to yourself, I am not going to bother reading any further because this book will not move me, I have a request. Please read the postscript before you give up. Then decide whether to resume this journey. If, instead, you are willing to continue reading already, then feel free to ignore the postscript entirely!

I repeat that postscript here.

"The thoughts that I am going to be expressing here did not occur to me, at least not fully formed, until some four years after I finished writing the original book and three years after the publication of the first edition."

"Shortly after publication, a college classmate of mine read the first edition and wrote to me with his comments. After the obligatory compliments, he stated that he thought 'an implicit assumption underlying the book was a need to attribute meaning.' I was mildly offended, perceiving a smugness lurking behind the comment."

"...Indeed, I certainly had not believed, nor would I admit, that such a 'need' was an implicit assumption underlying my work."

"...Over the following three years, I thought repeatedly about his comment and my reaction to it. I also reread the book several times (resulting, by the way, for unrelated reasons, in new, heavily revised versions). I think that I now see clearly, from my (obviously biased) perspective, what had happened while I was originally writing it.

"I began the project with the simple goals stated in the preface—to understand what it is about the world that we actually know and what the open questions are, with the prejudices disclosed. I believe that I had, in fact, made no assumptions about meaning when I started. However, as the work progressed, I found myself regularly stumbling over, bumping into or accidentally uncovering glimpses of things that suggested the existence of meaning in our Universe.

"In rereading what I wrote, I noticed that the tone gradually changed from the first to the last chapter, going from relatively objective, analytical and dry to more expansive, speculative and, what I hope I can call, almost lyrical. The changes in tone reflect what I now view as the my 'progress' on a journey of discovery and awakening—the gradual, growing realization of the possibility of something more; something that transcends our normal reality; something, in fact, that might make sense of the existence (and consequent experience) of anticipation, wonder, joy, curiosity, aspiration, integrity and artistic expression; something that might even explain hope, laughter, tears and love.

"What it is, I cannot say. But, its presence is dogged and pervasive. And, my increasing awareness of it affected, and was reflected in, my writing.

"For a new version, I contemplated revising the entire approach of the book (and the title) to be explicitly a story of 'the discovery of the possibility of purpose and meaning'. But, I rejected that approach as weakening what I actually already had. The book as originally written documented and revealed, both in content and in tone, the stages of my journey. That story, I did not want to lose. My revisions may have heightened what was happening but have not change it.

"With the book continuing in this form, I hope that you can experience this journey more or less as I did."

The progression in that writing seemed almost linear, continuous. My subsequent writings, in contrast, tend to, well, meander. To wander. But, that does not mean that they do not, in the aggregate, point. A few steps this way, a few that way, forward, backward; but, still heading somewhere in the end.

But, heading where?

For context, I use quotations from two writers out of books that I have already discussed above.

First, Nicholas Humphrey; second, Thomas Hertog.

I.

"Thomas Mann, in an essay on 'What I believe', wrote: 'In my deepest soul I hug the supposition that with God's "Let there be", which summoned the cosmos out of nothing, and with the generation of life from the inorganic, it was man who was ultimately intended.... . **Whether that be so or not, it would be as well for man to behave as if it were so.**'

...

"[S]uppose he had written 'it was phenomenal consciousness [sentience] that was ultimately intended, and with this a great experiment was initiated, the failure of which would be the failure of creation itself.' I could go with that.** Even if the idea of a naturally evolved feature being 'intended' must be wrong, I imagine that Darwin himself could have seen phenomenal consciousness as an 'ultimate' achievement—the crowning glory of the evolutionary process that began with the Big Bang. It's an invention so sublime that, if it were to cease to exist, it would indeed diminish the whole of creation."

Sentience, p.213 (emphasis added).

I have problems with the emphasis on "sentience." The categories of phenomenal and cognitive consciousness do not capture what is important.

Sentience refers to experiencing feelings or sensations as a result of sensory stimulation. Fine. But, I think that the most significant feelings are those of awe, wonder, joy, love. These feelings have some connection to sensory inputs, but reflect something else. We can be moved by music, but the feelings do not arise out of individual notes or sounds. We can be moved by language, but the emotions are not primarily the result of auditory and visual inputs. They are caused by the contents of the communication. Then, we have imagination, the "thirst" for knowledge or adventure, the hoped for feelings of fulfillment or satisfaction or achievement. These all are part of consciousness. Indeed, they are the part that is so special. If we substituted these capacities for "phenomenal consciousness" in the quotation, then I would whole-heartedly agree:

> "[A]n invention so sublime that, if it were to cease to exist,
> it would indeed diminish the whole of creation.
> I could go with that."

II.

Hertog:

"Our top-down perspective reverses the hierarchy between laws and reality in physics. It leads to a new philosophy of physics that rejects the idea that the universe is a machine governed by unconditional laws with a prior existence and replaces it with the view that **the universe is a kind of self-organizing entity, in which all sorts of emergent patterns appear,** the most general of which we call the laws of physics. ...The theory holds that **if there is an answer to the great question of existence, it is to be found within this world, not in a structure of absolutes beyond it.**"

On the Origin of Time: Stephen Hawking's Final Theory (2023), p.258 (emphasis added):

I do not think that Hertog/Hawking, nor science in general, have established this proposition about the "great question of existence." They certainly have not persuaded me. Not that I know that there is something important beyond this world, but I do know that science cannot explain very significant aspects of this world and cannot demonstrate that there is nothing more.

I am not arguing that we we can find "God in the gaps" (I find that disparaging characterization to be disingenuous, at best—the "gaps" are fundamental). It is simply that I believe that what science does not know provides far greater insights into and is much more relevant to the "great question of existence" than what is known.

*   *   *

Me?

I end up with simply this:

There is more than just what I can see—a more that matters,
one that is relevant to our life and existence—as a result of which
humankind has a fundamental place and a central role
as a source of meaning in the Universe.

That, I believe.

"You know I'm more and more convinced
The longer that I live
Yeah, this can't be... no, this can't be
No, this can't be all there is...."

...

"They tell me that there's more to life
than just what I can see.
I believe. Oh, I... I believe"

Brooks & Dunn
"Believe" (2005)

Books

Baoshu, *The Redemption of Time* (2016).

Cester, Clemente, and Korff, *Newton and Relativity.*

Carroll, Sean M., The Big Picture: On the Origins of Life, Meaning, and *the Universe Itself* (2016).

Carroll, Sean M., *The Biggest Ideas in the Universe: Space, Time, and Motion* (2023).

Cox, Brian, and Jeff Forshaw, *Why Does E=mc²? (And Why Should We Care?)* (2009).

Frankopan, Peter, *The Earth Transformed: An Untold History* (2023).

Hands, John, *Cosmosapiens: Human Evolution from the Origin of the Universe* (2016).

Hertog, Thomas, *On the Origin of Time: Stephen Hawking's Final Theory* (2023).

Hoel, Erik, *The World Behind the World: Consciousness, Free Will, and the Limits of Science* (2023).

Hossenfelder, Sabine, *Lost in Math: How Beauty Leads Physics Astray* (2018).

Humphrey, Nicholas, *Sentience: The Invention of Consciousness* (2023).

Jaynes, Julian, *The Origin of Consciousness in the Breakdown of the Bicameral Mind* (1976, 1990) (2000 edition).

Krauss, Lawrence, *The Edge of Knowledge: Unsolved Mysteries of the Cosmos* (2023).

Kronman, Anthony T., *After Disbelief: On Disenchantment, Disappointment, Eternity, and Joy* (2022).

McCarthy, Cormac, *Stella Maris* (2022).

McCarthy, Cormac, *The Passenger* (2022).

Mukherjee, Siddhartha, *The Song of the Cell: An Exploration of Medicine and the New Human* (2022).

Parisi, Giorgio, *In a Flight of Starlings: The Wonders of Complex Systems* (2023).

Pinker, Steven, *Rationality: What It Is, Why It Seems Scarce, Why It Matters* (2021).

Rovelli, Carlo, *The Order of Time* (2016).

Sapolsky, Robert M., *Determined: A Science of Life without Free Will* (2023).

Schrödinger, Erwin, "What is Life? The Physical Aspect of the Living Cell" (first published in 1944).

Wilczek, Frank, *Fundamentals: Ten Keys to Reality* (2021).

Articles/Chapters

Allen, Colin, and Neal Jacob, "Teleological Notions in Biology," *The Stanford Encyclopedia of Philosophy* (Spring 2020 Edition).

Ball, Philip, "Life does not run like clockwork," *CHEMISTRYWORLD*, 16 March 2022.

Caldwell, Luke, "The Mystery of Matter," *Scientific American Magazine*, February 2024.

Chiang, Ted, "Story of Your Life," *Arrival* (2016), originally published as *Stories of Your Life and Others* (2002).

Chown, Marcus, "Newton vs Einstein: what is the major discrepancy between their theories of gravity?" *BBC Sky at Night Magazine*, 19 January 2024 (originally appeared in the December 2006).

Dewhurst, Joe, "Causal Emergence and Real Patterns," *philsci-archive.pitt.edu*, April 3, 2020.

Dunham, Will, "Scientists discover that universe is awash in gravitational," *Reuters*, June 29, 2023.

erikweijers,"Summary of the Origin of Consciousness," posted 29 September 2014.

Feyman, Richard, "Optics: The Principle of Least Time," *Feynman Lectures*, Vol. 1, No. 26 (1963, 2013).

Fowler, Michael, University of Virginia, *Modern Physics*.

Garisto, Dan, "LK-99 isn't a superconductor—how science sleuths solved the mystery: Efforts to replicate the material have pieced together the puzzle of why it displayed superconducting-like behaviours," *Nature*, 16 August 2023.

Gupta, Rajendra, "How old is the universe exactly? A new theory suggests that it's been around for twice as long as believed," *The Conversation*, August 28, 2023.

Lee, Sukbae, Ji-Hoon Kim and Young-Wan Kwon, "The First Room-Temperature Ambient-Pressure Superconductor," submitted 22 July 2023.

Liu, Jerry Z., "The Simplest Derivation of E=mc2," Stanford University (1998).

Mack, Katie, "Many questions remain unanswered when it comes to matter, but the biggest one is: Why is there any matter to begin with?" *BBC Science Focus*, New Year Issue, December 2023.

Moore, James W., "Volition in Jaynes' The Origin of Consciousness …," *Frontiers in Psychology*, December 20, 2021.

Ogasa, Nikk, "Recoiling black holes could move at nearly one-tenth the speed of light: The cosmic sinkholes gain speed from being kicked by gravitational waves," *ScienceNews*, August 18, 2023.

Overbye, Dennis, "Black Holes May Hide a Mind-Bending Secret About Our Universe," *NYT.com*, October 12, 2022.

Rizk, Bernard, "New research puts age of universe at 26.7 billion years, nearly twice as old as previously believed," *phys.org* , July 13, 2023.

Siegel, Ethan, "Ask Ethan: Do JWST's results contradict the Big Bang? JWST has brought us more distant views of the early Universe than ever before. Is the Big Bang, and all of modern cosmology, in trouble?," *Starts With A Bang*, April 21, 2023.

Siegel, Ethan, "Is the Universe 13.8 or 26.7 billion years old?" *Big Think: Starts with a Bang*, July 18, 2023.

Specktor, Brandon, "13 billion-year-old 'Maisie's galaxy' is one of the oldest objects in the universe, James Webb telescope reveals," *Live Science*, August 17, 2023.

Strickland, Ashley, "Webb telescope captures image of most distant star ever seen," *CNN*, August 11, 2023.

Physics LibreTexts, "9.4: Resistivity and Resistance ," *phys.libre-texts.org*, September 12, 2022.

University Physics, Volume 2, "9.2 Model of Conduction in Metals," *OpenStax*.

University Physics, Volume 2, "9.3 Resistivity and Resistance," *OpenStax*.

University of Cambridge, "Dissemination of IT for the Promotion of Materials Science." *doItpoms.ac.uk*.

Zimmerman Jones, Andrew, "Voltage Definition in Physics," *ThoughtCo*, updated January 28, 2019.

John majored in economics at Amherst College, receiving a BA in 1970. He received his JD from The Harvard Law School in 1973. Following law school, he did post-graduate research at Trinity College, University of Cambridge. In late 1974, John began a 37-year career as a commercial litigator with a major law firm in New York City. He retired from the practice of law in 2011, after which he relocated to a small village outside of Cambridge, England. In March 2015, however, John was diagnosed with ALS (motor neuron disease). As a result, he decided to return to the U.S., to live in Old Town Alexandria, Virginia, with his daughter Sarah. His son John Eliot and daughter-in-law Megan, with his two grandchildren Hannah and Jeffrey, live nearby. Confined to a wheelchair since 2018, he has been writing.

Other Books by John E. Beerbower

Important Things We Don't Know (About Nearly Everthing)

Wanderings of a Captive Mind

The Eyes Have It (Wanderings Part 2)

All that Is Gold (Wanderings Part 3)

On Living While Dying: A Decade with ALS

Still Wandering: Still Wondering (Wanderings Part 4)

Politics, History and Ideology: Fruit of Forced Idleness

Disappointments (Wanderings Part 5)